RABBI AKIVA

כְּמָה לָקוּ בָּאֶצְבַּע עֶשֶׂר מַכּוֹת
אֱמֹר מֵעַתָּה בְּמִצְרַיִם
לָקוּ עֶשֶׂר מַכּוֹת

רַבִּי אֱלִיעֶזֶר
וְעַל הַיָּם לָקוּ חֲמִשִּׁים מַכּוֹת
אוֹמֵ' מִנַּיִן שֶׁכָּל מַכָּה וּמַכָּה
שֶׁהֵבִיא הַקָּדוֹשׁ בָּרוּךְ הוּא עַל

הַמִּצְרִיִּים בְּמִצְרַיִם הָיְתָה שֶׁל אַרְבַּע מַכּוֹ[ת]
שֶׁנֶּאֱ' יְשַׁלַּח בָּם חֲרוֹן אַפּוֹ עֶבְרָה וָזַעַם וְצָרָה
מִשְׁלַחַת מַלְאֲכֵי רָעִים עֶבְרָה אַחַת וָזַעַם
שְׁתַּיִם צָרָה שָׁלֹשׁ מִשְׁלַחַת מַלְאֲכֵי רָעִים
אַרְבַּע אֱמֹר מֵעַתָּה בְּמִצְרַיִם לָקוּ אַרְבָּעִים
מַכּוֹת וְעַל הַיָּם לָקוּ מָאתַיִם מַכּוֹת

רַבִּי עֲקִיבָא
אוֹמֵר מִנַּיִן שֶׁכָּל
מַכָּה וּמַכָּה שֶׁהֵבִ[יא]

Rabbi Akiva

Sage of the Talmud

◆◦◆

BARRY W. HOLTZ

Yale

UNIVERSITY

PRESS

New Haven and London

Yale University Press books may be purchased in quantity for educational, business, or promotional use. For information, please e-mail sales.press@yale.edu (U.S. office) or sales@yaleup.co.uk (U.K. office).

Set in Janson Oldstyle type by Integrated Publishing Solutions.
Printed in the United States of America.

Frontispiece: A page from the "Rylands Haggadah" (mid-fourteenth century) containing the debate about the number of plagues at the time of the Exodus. Rabbi Eliezer is represented seated above in the right-hand margin, and Rabbi Akiva is below. Akiva's face is obscured due to flaking of the paint over time. (Copyright of the University of Manchester)

Library of Congress Control Number: 2016951997
ISBN 978-0-300-20487-2 (cloth : alk. paper)

A catalogue record for this book is available from the British Library.

This paper meets the requirements of ANSI/NISO Z39.48-1992 (Permanence of Paper).

10 9 8 7 6

To Art Green
For fifty-five years of friendship
Long may it continue

There's the story, then there's the real story, then there's the story of how the story came to be told. Then there's what you leave out of the story. Which is part of the story too.
—Margaret Atwood, *MaddAddam*

CONTENTS

ACKNOWLEDGMENTS

THIS BOOK OWES its origins to an accidental convergence of events. In the midst of a dinner with a group of people at a restaurant in Palo Alto the evening before a lecture I was giving at Stanford, Steve Zipperstein was describing some of the forthcoming books in the Jewish Lives series. In passing I mentioned that I had, a few years before, thought of writing a book about Rabbi Akiva, though I didn't think it was likely to be of interest to most trade publishers and I had never pursued it. The day after my talk, much to my surprise Steve came up to me and said, "I'd love to talk to you about your Akiva idea." At the time I was the dean of the William Davidson Graduate School of Jewish Education at the Jewish Theological Seminary, and I told him that at this point I couldn't possibly do it—just being dean was so time consuming that my writing mostly consisted of grant proposals and memos. "How about this?" he said. "I've wanted to have an Akiva book in the series, and

I'd really like you to present a proposal. If someone else comes along, I'll let you have the right of first refusal. In the meanwhile I'll hold on to the idea until you're ready to try your hand at it." Two years later, when I was finishing my five years as dean, I emailed Steve. "You still have first crack at it," he replied. "Write me a proposal." So that's how this book came to be part of the Jewish Lives series. My deep and abiding gratitude goes to Steve for his patience and persistence and for giving me the chance to work on such a deeply engaging project.

Thanks as well to the many people at Yale University Press, particularly those involved with this series—among them John Palmer, Linda C. Kurz, Ileene Smith, Erica Hanson, and Jessie Dolch—who have been so professional and such a pleasure to work with.

I am grateful to my home base, the Jewish Theological Seminary, for granting me a sabbatical leave in the year following the conclusion of my deanship. This gave me the necessary time to start the research and writing for this book. Over the past three years I have had a number of opportunities to teach some of the texts explored in this book in a variety of settings—in my courses at JTS, at a variety of synagogues, at the conference of Network for Research in Jewish Education, and with participants in the Mandel Teacher Educator Institute. Virtually every time I teach these materials, I am fortunate to gain new insights from the comments of the students in those classes. Through teaching, my own understanding of Akiva has grown over time, and I thank those many students from whom I have learned such a great deal.

If I listed every person I know who expressed interest in and offered encouragement about this book over these past three years, the list would go on for far too many pages. I am grateful to all of those friends and colleagues even though I don't have space to name each of you individually. I do want to mention a few people with whom I had regular and ongoing conversations or who offered advice about specific issues that came up in the course of the project. Many thanks to Larry Fine, Benjamin Gampel, Art Green, Ed Greenstein, Daniel Marom, Sharon Liberman Mintz, Robert Prince, Nessa Rapoport, Jeffrey Rubenstein, and George Savran. My thanks also to Lucia Pizarro Wehlen, a rabbinical student at JTS, who served as my research assistant during the first six months of my work on the book.

Three friends went beyond the call of duty in helping me think about this project. I am grateful to Richard Kalmin and Seth Schwartz, whose great knowledge about this field helped guide me through the maze of scholarship both on rabbinic sources and on the historical context of Akiva's world. They suggested numerous books and articles for me to explore and answered my interminable questions patiently and with good humor.

During the year I was on sabbatical, virtually every Monday morning my friend Michael Paley and I sat together in my dining room studying Akiva texts together, trying to dive into the stories and the teachings associated with this remarkable figure from long ago who played such a crucial role in the earliest days of the evolution of Judaism. Reading these texts with Michael, puzzling over them, arguing over them, was truly the best way to launch this project, and I am grateful to him both for his interpretative acumen and for the good times we had conversing together.

As always I am delighted by my children Sophia and Elan, who help keep my eye on the big picture of things and who had the good grace to no longer be living at home while I was writing this book! And finally, to my wife Bethamie Horowitz. I don't think that Bethamie ever counted on living three years of her marriage with a third member of the marital household—a two-thousand-year-old rabbinic sage who seemed to occupy an awful lot of my conversation. My eternal thanks to her for putting up with this elderly visitor.

Akiva's life, as I try to show in this book, is profoundly bound up in the world of teachers and students, and in that light it is hard for me not to note the passing of four of my own teachers since my last book appeared a few years ago. Joseph Lukinsky, Seymour Fox, Allen Grossman, and Jesper Rosenmeier are no longer with us. Their influence, as Akiva would well have known, remains forever with me. On a much happier note, I am truly fortunate that one of my dear teachers is still teaching and writing and inspiring his students. It is to him that I dedicate this book.

RABBI AKIVA

Introduction

CONSIDER FOR A MOMENT the following thought experiment. Let us think of the Babylonian Talmud not as we usually do—not as a vast compendium of laws, legends, debates, and interpretations, but rather as a massive, multivolume, postmodern experimental novel. Wilder than *Moby-Dick*, beyond the imagination of James Joyce, more internally self-referential than anything dreamed up by David Foster Wallace. Hundreds of pages of dialogue, of discussions that start but never end; organized, it seems on the surface, by free association, and filled with hyperlinked cross-references across the wide expanse of its domain. It has no beginning and no conclusion. It just *is*. It is as if the Talmud expects that you have read it all before you've read a single page.

In this novel, as in any novel, there are settings. Here there are real places with real names: Jerusalem, Bene-Berak, and

Tiberias—all in Eretz Yisrael, or the Land of Israel—as well as Egypt, Babylonia, and Rome. There are stories—some miraculous, some quite mundane. And there are characters—farmers and merchants, priests and Romans, women and children, slaves and free people. And most of all there are rabbis—rabbis who constantly talk and debate and prod one another to greater feats of argumentation. It is their world, the landscape of rabbis, that most dominates this novel. And amid all this excess, all these words and characters, if we were to ask, "Who is the hero of this extraordinary book, who is its central figure?" I think—despite the vastness of the work, it's not such a difficult question to answer—it is Rabbi Akiva,[1] a "father of the world," as the Jerusalem Talmud calls him.

In many ways Akiva is the apotheosis of the deepest values of "rabbinic Judaism," the essential manifestation of Jewish religion that first evolved in the first and second centuries of the Common Era and came to define the nature of Judaism for hundreds of years. And indeed, the essence of rabbinic Judaism, despite its various incarnations and expressions, is what many people mean by "Judaism" today. This is a religion based on God's Torah and the various interpretations of that Torah as adduced by rabbis over the course of centuries. The Torah, in this conception, owes its authority to God and, thanks to its divine origins, contains within it myriad possibilities and unimaginable depths.

The Torah and the rabbis who interpreted it have laid out a system of commandments (called "mitzvot") that influence virtually every aspect of a person's life—prayer, festivals both solemn and joyous, interpersonal ethics, rules about eating, matters of civil and criminal law, and much more. The rabbi acts as interpreter of Torah as well as judge and scholar, preacher and public leader. In Akiva's time, these functions were just beginning to evolve, and some did not manifest themselves for generations.[2] Rabbis, for example, were not yet leaders of the community; they were by and large a fairly small, elite, and separate group. (The word "rabbi" in its etymological core simply means "my master" and connotes more of the teacher or mentor function of the role in its origins.)[3] But the seeds of this future were first sown in Akiva's lifetime, and he had much to do with what we have come to know as rabbinic Judaism.

As important as these early sages were, I suspect that if today you asked someone with even a moderate connection to Judaism to name one rabbi from ancient times, it is unlikely that he or she would come up with any name *aside* from Akiva. (A few might suggest Maimonides, but he is a figure from medieval times, not the ancient world; and others might suggest Hillel, but he essentially is a precursor to Akiva's world and certainly was never called "rabbi.") Perhaps Akiva's name recognition is related to the fact that he is known from the Passover Haggadah, or perhaps it is because the story of his death is so disturbingly brutal, or perhaps it is because he appears as an important figure in so many stories of the early period of Judaism—stories retold so often that, in the words of the Talmud scholar Beth Berkowitz, they "seem to constitute a new Jewish core curriculum."[4] Akiva always seems to be in the middle of the action, whether he is the central player himself or a significant supporting actor.

He is the interpreter of Torah so acute that every detail of the text holds secret meanings. If he was not the very first to push interpretation to such heights, he surely was one of the first, and he is certainly the most well-known and imaginative. He becomes the model for Jewish intellectual creativity, at least in its religious form, for almost two thousand years. More than that, Akiva is the *teacher* par excellence, the image of what it means to be a rabbi. And, finally, in the manner of his dying—tortured to death by the Roman authorities for his insistence

3

on teaching Torah in public—he became the model for the rest of Jewish history of what it means to be a martyr.

What does it mean to write a "biography" of a figure from so long ago? And what does the concept of "biography" mean as we see it played out in the literature of the ancient rabbis?

To begin with let us consider the sources of material about Akiva. The time we are speaking of is often called the "Rabbinic Period" or the "Talmudic Age," and it refers, more or less, to the first six centuries of the Common Era (CE).[5] Akiva's life overlapped the first two centuries of that age. This coincided with a time of Roman rule in ancient Israel (and Roman rule continued well after his death), and it includes two of the most dramatic events in all of Jewish history: the Romans' destruction of the Jewish Temple and Jerusalem (70 CE), and the failed revolt against Rome (132–135 CE) led by a figure known as Bar Kokhba.

The stories about Akiva and his pronouncements about law, ethics, and theology are collected in literary works that came into existence many years after his time. Those works (often called the "Oral Torah" since these teachings were transmitted orally long before they were written down; as opposed to the "Written Torah," namely, the Bible) include, among others, the Mishnah, the first great work of rabbinic Judaism (ca. 220 CE), and the Babylonian Talmud (ca. 600 CE; the word "Talmud" means "study"), which incorporates almost the entire Mishnah and is structured as a kind of lengthy expansion of and commentary on the Mishnah.[6] Where the Mishnah is short, pithy, prescriptive, and somewhat elusive as to its intentions, the Talmud is discursive and filled with argumentation and discussions of reasoning; yet often it is inconclusive in its determination of the resolution of the issue at hand.[7]

In fact in the rabbinic library there are two Talmuds. Besides the Babylonian Talmud (abbreviated as "b." in references), there is the one known in Hebrew as the Talmud Yerushalmi (abbreviated as "y." in references), translated variously as "the Jerusalem Talmud," "the Talmud of the Land of Israel," or (generally in older references) "the Palestinian Talmud." The Jerusalem Talmud (ca. 400 CE) is shorter and was composed in the Land of Israel (though not in Jerusalem). Because Akiva lived in Palestine, texts preserved in the Jerusalem Talmud are particularly relevant to our project here: we can see materials somewhat closer to his own lifetime and traditions emanating from the Land of Israel rather than from Babylonia. (Of course, all of these works evolved and developed over the course of many years before they reached the form in which we have them today, so giving the works a precise date is somewhat misleading.)

Aside from scholars, particularly academic scholars, people generally have been far less interested in the Jerusalem Talmud throughout Jewish history than in the Babylonian Talmud. When people talk about "the Talmud," they are almost always referring to the Babylonian Talmud. This is the massive work that students and rabbis have spent generations commenting upon, discussing, debating, and extolling. In addition, there are texts about Akiva found in collections of midrashim (plural of "midrash," a word meaning "search out" or "interpret"), which are commentaries (ca. 300 CE and onward) on the Bible. Akiva was truly a master of midrash, and many of his interpretative insights and stories about him are found in these collections. (Contrary to its popular usage, there is no single work called "the Midrash," but rather a variety of ancient anthologies of these teachings.) A good portion of the Babylonian Talmud is devoted to debates about Jewish law (civil, criminal, and ritual), but alongside those materials are midrashic commentaries on biblical passages, discussions of magic and health, parables, and many stories about the rabbis themselves.

As the study of the Talmud moved into the world of university scholarship beginning in the nineteenth century and continuing to our own times, academic scholars began to explore the questions that historians generally raise about ancient materials. These approaches differ enormously from the classic modes of Talmud study found in the religious world of the Beit Midrash—the "house of study," or yeshiva (talmudic academy). Among the questions that history-oriented or literary-minded scholars have raised are those relating to the dating of various talmudic sources and the way that the Talmud was edited and structured. Both Talmuds are organized into large volumes, based on the divisions in the Mishnah, called "tractates," each of which bears a title that represents the main focus of each book. But discussions, stories, and themes range far and wide and are not well-defined by the title of the volume. Indeed, the Hebrew word used for "tractate," *masekhet*, literally means "web," and a web of associations and connections is as good a description of the talmudic tractate as one can find. As I quote from talmudic sources in this book, I first give the name of the tractate (sometimes preceded by the abbreviation "y." or "b." to indicate the Jerusalem or Babylonian Talmud, respectively), followed by a translation of the tractate's name the first time it appears in a chapter, and then a page number (for example: Nedarim "Vows" 62b).[8]

Two additional terms will be helpful to know. The sages who were responsible for producing and promulgating the traditions up to and including the Mishnah are known as the Tannaim (plural of Tanna, "repeater" or "teacher"), and those responsible for producing the later materials (such as both the Jerusalem and Babylonian Talmuds) are known as Amoraim (plural of Amora, "discusser"). Hence the Rabbinic Period can be neatly divided into two segments: the Tannaitic and Amoraic periods, with the redaction of the Mishnah as the watershed event, though of course Tannaim aplenty appear in the Amoraic works.[9]

This literature contains a wide array of materials, heavily emphasizing legal debates and rulings,[10] but also including a myriad number of stories—some in the form of parables, some as what we might call "cases," and many being narratives about the lives of the rabbis whose utterances fill the pages of these volumes. Thus many "biographical" fragments are scattered throughout these works that, pieced together, might give us the life story of Akiva. And for centuries that is precisely how these stories were viewed—as presenting a life story. In the past forty years or so, however, this traditional understanding has been challenged. Scholars have questioned whether "biography" is at all the right category to apply to these tales from the Rabbinic Period.

Three questions have been raised about viewing this literature as biography. First, the concept of "biography" that we have today is closely related to our notion of history. Namely, biography is the factually accurate representation of real events. Of course biographers can bring various scholarly perspectives to this work. One can be a Freudian biographer or a Marxist-oriented biographer or a biographer with a strong feminist perspective. But these are only the *frames* that might be applied to the work. The underlying commitment to historical accuracy, as best as it can be achieved, drives the biographer's task in all cases. But is that what the rabbis of the past meant by their version of biographical storytelling?

There are times when the rabbinic stories *do* seem very close to real life, but there are also miracle stories or stories that are hardly credible from a historical point of view. What are we to make of a story told in the Babylonian Talmud in which the sage R. Joshua ben Hananiah[11] enters into a debate with the emperor of Rome's daughter (b. Hullin "Ordinary Animal Sacrifices" 60a)? Or the story in which Rabban Yohanan ben Zakkai[12] meets the Roman general Vespasian and predicts that Vespasian will soon become the emperor of Rome (b. Gittin

"Decrees of Divorce" 58a–b)? Joshua ben Hananiah was Akiva's teacher and Yohanan ben Zakkai was one of the greatest rabbinic teachers at the time of Akiva's youth. Is it at all credible that they would have had conversations with Roman generals and the children of emperors?

The concern for historical accuracy that we see today as essential to biography seems not to have been a matter of interest to the ancient storytellers. Thus a number of contemporary scholars prefer to view the rabbinic tales as closer to literature than they are to biography. Indeed, at times the individual narratives seem like quite sophisticated and well-wrought short stories with thematic coherence and elements of literary symbolism.

The person who probably was most responsible for setting the agenda for new ways to think about rabbinic stories is the influential American Talmud scholar Jacob Neusner. In a lecture delivered in 1980, Neusner laid out a challenge to viewing these narratives as matters of history. According to Neusner, historians have been asking the wrong questions about these tales. Instead of "asking what really 'happened' behind a story (the kernel of truth)," we should be looking to what these tales tell us about the culture that produced them. These stories are "not an account of one-time events, history in the old sense"; rather, they show us the "persistent traits of social culture and mind" of the rabbinic world.[13] These "biographical" stories, then, should be seen as a window onto a world from the past, not a narrative of actual events. We cannot know for sure, in other words, whether this or that event happened in Akiva's life; we can only investigate the cultural meaning of preserving these stories for the future.

At around the same time as Neusner was writing in the United States, Yonah Fraenkel, a scholar at the Hebrew University in Jerusalem, was offering his own critique of the traditional approach to these stories with a slightly different slant from Neusner's. Rather than Neusner's cultural historical approach to the biographical tales, Fraenkel takes a much more *literary* stance. Read them as *stories*, he says—as works of fiction, not as stories trying to be reliable biography.[14]

It is interesting to note that for most of the history of talmudic study—certainly in the classic yeshivot—the *stories* in the pages of the Talmud were considered hardly interesting at all, except perhaps where they indicated the legal practice of a particular rabbi.[15] The stories were the parts of the text that one moved through quickly so that one could get to what *really* mattered—the debates and arguments in all their subtle detail that seemed to be at the heart of the talmudic enterprise. But perhaps because we live in a time in which the narrative mode of thinking has become so compelling,[16] those neglected stories of the rabbinic world have gained a great deal of traction among writers and scholars from a broad range of perspectives.

The contemporary scholar most associated with work on rabbinic stories is Jeffrey L. Rubenstein, who has laid out in a number of influential and important works a clear-eyed and comprehensive approach to reading these texts.[17] Rabbinic texts, as Rubenstein shows, are wonderfully ambiguous, open to a variety of methodologies and interpretive readings. Rubenstein is not alone in approaching these materials in this way; other contemporary scholars bring a similar perspective to the stories about the sages. Following in the footsteps of Neusner and Fraenkel these writers relate to the materials not as historical data but as literary and cultural footprints from the rabbinic past.[18] My reading in this book of the stories about Akiva follows in this same tradition.

A second important element to consider is that rabbinic literature does not present coherent, compact, birth-to-death narratives of rabbis' lives. Instead, the stories about Akiva, for example, are scattered throughout the pages of various rabbinic texts. In that way, rabbinic "biography" is quite unlike another literature from a closely related time period—Greek and Roman biography, particularly as we see it in the works of Plutarch, who lived almost at the same time as Akiva.

In his *Lives*, Plutarch gives us a series of short (thirty to fifty pages each, in English translation) mini-biographies of the great figures of Greek and Roman culture. Of course, I am not suggesting that Plutarch's *Lives* hewed to the standards of modern biography either. Plutarch did have an agenda, and no one would claim that his portraits are historically reliable in the modern sense of the word. As one scholar has put it, "Plutarch's overriding purpose is to bring out the moral pattern in his hero's career."[19] Plutarch presents only one example of a whole genre of biographical literature from the world of the distant past. As a whole, Rubenstein writes: "Ancient biographers did not intend to present the 'true' life of their subject—the life as actually lived. . . . They sought 'truth' in a different sense, the eternal truths that the meaning of the life of their subject held for others. The biographers constructed their subjects such that the lives embodied the values they wished to impart to their audience."[20]

But what we do get with Plutarch's *Lives* is a series of organized narratives, very different from the biographies of the rabbis in the Talmud and other sources, that the reader must piece together from disparate strands. Indeed, rather than using the term "biography" to describe rabbinic literature, we might say that we are presented with "anecdotes"—fragments of a life. To tell the story of Akiva's life, we must stitch together stories from different parts of the rabbinic canon, stories that sometimes contradict one another. That contrast with Plutarch helps us see in bold relief a critique of rabbinic tales as biography that might be called the problem of *coherence*. Let's say there are thirty stories about a rabbinic figure (there are many more about Akiva), and on top of that we have legal opinions and teachings identified with the same rabbi—for instance, a story about how the rabbi dealt with a difficult student in class, a story about what time of day the rabbi said particular prayers, an interpretation of a biblical verse, a ruling about how a case of property damage should be adjudicated. And these stories come from various places in the map of rabbinic literature. How much can we really say that every story and every teaching attributed to this particular rabbi represents that rabbi's life and views? If we cannot rely on any particular story being about any particular rabbi, this argument goes, how can we use these tales to construct a biography?

Finally, another challenge about constructing rabbinic biography is related to the sources of information upon which we must rely. Essentially, everything we know about Akiva comes from the *internal* sources of Judaism—the Mishnah (abbreviated "m." in references) and Tosefta (a text from around the same time as the Mishnah and similar to it; abbreviated "t." in references), the two Talmuds, and the various midrashim. We don't have Akiva's letters or diaries or household records, tax receipts, or shopping lists. Akiva does not appear in official documents of the Roman authorities, nor is he mentioned in virtually any source outside of those within the Jewish world.[21] There is no particular reason to be surprised about this, of course. The Romans paid little attention to the Jewish individuals in Palestine, with a very few notable exceptions. In a certain sense Akiva (like virtually all of his contemporaries) is a man who was not there.

Nonetheless, Akiva is to be found throughout rabbinic literature; he's mentioned 1,341 times in the Babylonian Talmud alone and hundreds of times in the Jerusalem Talmud, the Tosefta, and the midrashic works of rabbinic Judaism. When looking at Akiva, we must turn to these texts, along with the contextual knowledge that historians and text scholars have provided over the course of many years of careful research. How we look at these "internal" Jewish sources will be an important consideration.

None of the discussion thus far is meant to say that Akiva was an imaginary figure, like the protagonists of novels. It's hard for me to believe that Akiva—and for that matter virtually all his contemporaries—was not a real human being. But of course I cannot prove that he was.[22]

Still, the weight of culture and tradition is powerful: I believe that Akiva and the other rabbis in his circle and after him lived in this world as much as I live in it today. I cannot know whether every story about him and every utterance attributed to him reflects what he did or said, but I do know that editors who established the texts that have come down to us from long ago chose to preserve certain stories and teachings in Akiva's name and that despite the complexities of transmission, it is possible to discern a portrait of his life. The more important question is not, "Did this event really happen?" but rather, "Why was it passed down?" and "What is it meant to communicate?"

The question remains: With all these impediments, what does it mean to write "biography" when biography hardly seems possible? To my mind the way to think about the present book is to see it as a kind of *imagined biography* rooted in the best that contemporary scholarship can teach us—about rabbinic tales, about Akiva himself, and about the historical context of the world of the rabbis in the first century and a half of the Common Era. This book brings with it a *self-reflective* stance and requires a certain modesty about the nature of this biographical enterprise. My goal is to consider the stories and teachings in the light of inner consistency on the one hand and a literary sensibility on the other while recognizing that the stories as we have received them cannot be understood naively as definitively factual. I read the stories about Akiva both as aspects of biography and as literary works expressing the culture, values, and religious teachings embedded in their texts. I will call the reader's attention to some of the issues related to the shaping and reshaping of the various texts over time, and I will call upon the work of academic scholars who concern themselves with these matters where they are relevant to our enterprise. But our focus will remain on the figure of Akiva as best we can uncover his life and personality.

In order to take seriously the insights of contemporary scholarship, I explore Akiva's life through an examination of a variety of rabbinic sources, putting these texts on the table, as it were, and reading them closely, in comparison and sometimes in contrast with other rabbinic sources. I have chosen to aim at a close reading of these texts because given what we know today about rabbinic biography as a genre, it is impossible to imagine writing a straightforward narrative of Akiva's life in the manner of the classic biography *Akiba: Scholar, Saint and Martyr* written by Louis Finkelstein some eighty years ago.[23] Finkelstein was a deeply learned scholar as well as a major leader in American Jewish life. His book exhibits his breadth of knowledge, but of course it is very much a work of its time. He did not have the benefit of perspectives on rabbinic tales that have emerged in the past quarter century and of the research on the world of ancient Near Eastern cultures that is available to us today. Moreover, Finkelstein's book is palpably shadowed by the Great Depression and the darkening days preceding the Second World War. Today his book reads more like a piece of historical fiction than a work of scholarship.[24]

It is interesting to note in that regard that the life of Akiva has occasioned some fascinating works of fiction, imagining his life particularly in relationship to the story of the "four who entered the orchard" (discussed in chapter 6) and imagining his relationship with Bar Kokhba (chapter 7). The most well-known of these fictional treatments is Milton Steinberg's *As a Driven Leaf*, in which Akiva is a central figure, though not the main protagonist.[25] Steinberg's book is not a great literary work, but it presents a cohesive portrait of the lives of the early rabbis and therefore has been taught with great pedagogic effect in innumerable classrooms since it first appeared in 1939. The Yiddish writer Joseph Opatoshu wrote a novelization of Akiva's life, *The Last Revolt*, focusing on Akiva's supposed connection to Bar Kokhba.[26] Unlike many fictionalized retellings of Akiva's life, Opatoshu's novel does not end with Akiva's martyrdom but with his shout of support for Bar Kokhba's messianic revolt. Howard Schwartz, a contemporary American poet and storyteller, published his version of the story in *The Four Who Entered Paradise*, with an additional twist, a "thematic commentary" by Marc Bregman, who is a contemporary midrash scholar.[27] The most recent fictionalization is a novel by the Israeli writer Yochi Brandes called *Akiva's Orchard* (it has not yet been translated into English).[28] Brandes brings inventive recastings of the Akivan stories and a feminist element into the traditional portrait. Doubtless there will be more works of fiction, as Akiva remains a fascinating figure.

It is no accident, I believe, that Akiva has inspired works of fiction—not only because of his importance in Jewish religious history, but also because of the simple fact that so many of the details of his life are unknown and therefore grist for the mill of a novelist. Just take the basic fact of when he lived. Conventionally, one will see the dates of his life given as between 50 and 135 CE, but we have no firm data about these numbers. This dating is really only speculation that comes from a bit of extrapolation. Namely, since the story of Akiva's death fits well with the persecutions following the failure of Bar Kokhba's revolt (explored in chapter 7), that death would make sense to occur around 135 CE, a historically reliable point close to the Bar Kokhba debacle. If we assume that Akiva lived to be a very old man, we merely subtract an eighty-five-year life from 135 CE and we have a birth date of 50 CE. It's guesswork and some arithmetic—not a definitive biographical fact.

Who were his parents? We know nothing about them,

which is not particularly surprising about his mother, given the patriarchal society of ancient times (though some significant female figures appear in rabbinic literature). But we know nothing about his father as well. Akiva is known as "Akiva the son of Joseph," but his father is not described in any rabbinic sources (despite the fact that if one peruses some books and online websites today, one will be assured that Akiva was the son or descendant of a convert—for which there is no evidence whatsoever).[29] And in fact, as Rubenstein points out, Akiva's name with his patronymic, "Akiva ben Yosef" in Hebrew, is a term that appears only around twelve times in all of the many references to Akiva in the Babylonian Talmud.[30]

We don't know where Akiva was born and even where he lived in later life. He is sometimes associated with the town of Bene-Berak, but that association derives from fewer than a handful of passing references in the literature. And finally, we do not know where he died or where he is buried. Most sources will state with assurance that he was executed and buried in the northern coastal city of Caesarea, but in fact the actual rabbinic stories about his execution—as we will see in chapter 7—do not mention the place where he died. The place of his death and burial is only a guess and not an established fact; it is not even attested in the talmudic sources.

Indeed, travel some fifty miles northeast of Caesarea and you will come to the ancient city of Tiberias, nestled alongside the large freshwater lake called Kinneret in Hebrew, the Sea of Galilee in English. Here you can be directed to the tomb of Rabbi Akiva—simple stone pillars with a white painted roof. It is a quiet place, open to the air, well-situated with a lovely view of the Kinneret—even, perhaps, a place for contemplation. What lies beneath the earth here? The actual final resting place of the sage? Historians would be right to cast a skeptical eye on such a claim. Yet pilgrims continue to arrive there. Like much about Rabbi Akiva, we remain caught between fact and legend, history and the shared memory of an old culture.

So then, why Akiva? Why should we care about this figure who lived two thousand years ago? I think it is because the story of his life is both archetypical and unique. It is easy to be drawn into the tale of his life. Born in poverty, unschooled in his religious tradition, he mocked scholars and disdained them (at least in one telling of his early life). But then a kind of religious revelation comes to him, and he decides that despite his advanced age he must learn Torah, starting from the very basics of the alphabet. And this man, enemy of scholars and profoundly ignorant, becomes the greatest rabbi of them all. As we will see, in another version of the story, he courts the daughter of a wealthy man—who opposes the relationship—and wins her heart and eventually the respect of her father through his learning. He is seen as both mystic and practical legal analyst, both theologian and text interpreter. He disputes with his colleagues in dramatic fashion, yet he is admired and beloved by his peers. And in the end, he becomes the exemplar of Jewish martyrs, executed by the Romans with the Shema, the central confession of Judaism, on his lips.

Before we turn to the stories and teachings that map out his life, we begin in chapter 1 by looking at the world into which Akiva was born. What were the realities of the time in which he lived? What were the political and social landscapes that would have been familiar to him? How have historians today come to view the context in which he lived? We begin with those questions.

A NOTE ON THE TRANSLATIONS OF THE TEXTS

I explore a variety of rabbinic sources in this book, all of course translations from Hebrew or Aramaic. Some of these

INTRODUCTION

translations—like the standard English translation of the Talmud and certain key midrashic texts published in the middle
of the twentieth century by Soncino Press—feel linguistically
rather old-fashioned. Others that are aimed at an academic audience trade ease of reading for the exactitude scholars require.
Such translations will often be filled with brackets, diacritical
marks in the transliteration of Hebrew words, and variant readings from divergent manuscript sources. These characteristics,
though admirable for their purposes, will not serve the needs of
a nonspecialist reader.

By and large, as is conventional practice, quotations from
the Hebrew Bible in this book use the current standard English
translation, *The Tanakh*, published by the Jewish Publication
Society, with a few small adaptations to fit the context in which
the Bible is being quoted.[31] Except where noted, I have translated all other Hebrew texts that we consider here, taking advantage of the resources offered by various existing translations
but trying to find the right combination of accessibility and accuracy. Because I engage in a kind of literary close reading of
many of these texts, I tried to be careful not to prejudice the
interpretation by adding elements that don't exist in the original source. Thus I've tried to keep to a minimum phrases one
will sometimes find in the Soncino translations such as "he exclaimed" where the original simply is "he said." And I have also
tried to translate the same word in a consistent fashion, at least
within an individual passage, so that readers can gauge the significance of repetitions that would be obscured by varying the
way a single word is translated.

I have made one concession for the sake of clarity: rabbinic
texts tend to use pronouns (or, in the manner of the Hebrew
language, pronouns that are embedded within verbs) rather
than repeat the name of the speaker. In the midst of a debate
in the Talmud it can be confusing to read "he said" followed by
"he said" and another "he said." In order to avoid confusion, I

have supplied the name of the speaker except in very rare cases where it seemed to me that the original text was being *intentionally* ambiguous.

Finally, one of the fascinating things about translating these texts is how quickly one notices the indeterminacy inherent in the nature of the Hebrew vocabulary these sources use. Rabbinic Hebrew has a smaller vocabulary than modern English, and therefore it is often difficult to determine which *precise* English word is appropriate to express the meaning of the text. In English we simply have a greater variety of words from which to choose. In one text that we will look at in chapter 2, for example, a key word might be translated as "carved," "hollowed out," or "engraved upon," and how one views the imprecise word might have a profound effect on how one reads the text. At times we can make a decent guess based on context, but at other times we have to be satisfied with an ambiguity that holds its own fascination.

1

Akiva's World

To UNDERSTAND Akiva's life we must try to understand something about the world in which he lived. This is not a simple task, however. We are speaking about a time almost two thousand years ago, and although historians have attempted to reconstruct that landscape, our sources are both constrained and contested. The Land of Israel was ruled by the Roman Empire, and Roman sources about Palestine, such as they are, view the world through Roman eyes.[1] Especially after the revolts of the Jews against the Romans, we can expect the ruling conqueror to be less than generous about the rebellious people who were conquered.[2]

Virtually all Jewish sources date from a time long after the first century of the Common Era—in some cases many hundreds of years later—and therefore are problematic as *historical* evidence. The most well-known contemporary information from that period comes from the Jewish historian Josephus, who managed to negotiate the boundaries of the Jewish and Roman worlds in a savvy and successful way. His works—taken with a degree of open-eyed wariness with which we must consider all premodern histories—remain a significant passageway into first-century Jewish life. Nonetheless, much remains uncertain, and scholars have argued over the *meaning* of events as much as they have about the narratives themselves. What was Jewish religious life like? Who were the leaders of the Jewish community? What rituals actually happened in the Temple, and what were the practices of ordinary Jews? There is much disagreement about these and many other questions. Still, enough evidence exists for historians to help us make sense of that time at least in its broad outlines.

As I have said, no one knows Akiva's birth date, and one can find a wide range of conjectures. As we have seen, most estimates appear to extrapolate back from the story of his death at the end of the Bar Kokhba War in 135 CE and estimate his birth to be around 50 CE. The precise date is not of consequence; far more important is the shared assumption that Akiva was born before the Great Revolt against Rome (66–70 CE) and therefore lived through what was surely the most cataclysmic event in Jewish history, at least until the Holocaust—the destruction of the Temple and Jerusalem in 70 CE. Every historical age might be said to be one of crisis and change, but in the history of the Jewish people, no time was more so than the first century of the Common Era.

But what of that world before the devastating end to the Great Revolt?

To understand the milieu into which Akiva was born we must go back to the conquests of Alexander the Great in the ancient Near East more than three hundred years before Akiva's time. Alexander died in 323 BCE, and in the aftermath of his death, the territories that he had conquered, including the Land of Israel, became the sites for years of conflict among various warring parties—descendants of his generals and their dynasties and descendants of the Jews known as the Maccabees (later called the Hasmoneans after a supposed ancestor) who in 167 BCE threw off the rule of one of the dynasties that emerged from Alexander's followers. This is the story at the heart of the holiday of Hanukkah.

The rule of the Hasmoneans was hardly a smooth one. Internal dissension, struggles for leadership, and essentially a full-scale civil war raged for some thirty years. All the while, lurking in the background, was the great power of the day—Rome, with ambitions for empire far beyond the dreams of any Hasmonean ruler. In the midst of the strife and confusion in Palestine, the Roman general Pompey moved into the Near East and captured Jerusalem in 63 BCE. This did not end the Hasmonean civil war; indeed, historians have argued that the internal conflicts within the *Roman* world exacerbated the situation in Palestine, with various figures in Rome supporting one side or the other in the civil war in Israel. Remember: on the world stage we are talking about the period in which Julius Caesar defeated this same Pompey in 48 BCE and was himself assassinated in 44 BCE. In fact, Mark Antony, well-known to us today thanks to Shakespeare, makes an appearance in our drama as well. His support of a wily young upstart named Herod led to Herod's being named king of the Jews by the Roman Senate in 40 BCE. By 37 BCE, Herod's military victories in Palestine solidified his status. He ruled in the Land of Israel for more than forty years.

Herod is an extraordinarily complex and fascinating character. He was a megalomaniac and paranoid despot, capable of great cruelty and violence. But at the same time he had a large vision for Israel with both the political connections in Rome and the iron will to realize his ambitions. Perhaps most of all Herod was a builder, and the products of his building projects are known to us even today. The city of Caesarea on the coast in the north of Israel and the fortresses of Herodium and Masada were all part of his building program. But the most important, the grandest, building project of Herod's career was the magnificent expansion of the Second Temple in Jerusalem.

The First Temple had been destroyed during the Babylonian conquest of Jerusalem in 586 BCE. Some eighty years later when exiled Jews in Babylonia were allowed to return to Israel to rejoin those who had remained there, a Second Temple of much diminished size was built. But Herod undertook a vast expansion—of both the city and the Temple. What he created was one of the greatest public buildings in the entire Roman Empire. Josephus called it "a structure more noteworthy than any in the world" (*Antiquities* 15:412).

During Herod's rule, Jerusalem became what we today would call a "destination travel site" for world Jewry—Jews flocked to the city for the great festivals of the liturgical year. The construction project took decades; in fact, the Temple was not completed until well after Herod's death. Thousands of jobs were created by the building enterprise, and money flowed into the city through the pilgrimage industry. Herod's Second Temple changed the *economic* status of Jerusalem.[3] All that changed again, as we will see, after the Great Revolt. But the Jerusalem that Akiva would have known (or heard about) in his youth was a wealthy city—a city busy with workers, filled with foreign visitors, and crowned by a magnificent building unlike anything else he would have experienced. Indeed, it was a cosmopolitan city, with Romans, other foreigners, and Jews from both Palestine and the Diaspora living in and visiting it. As one historian has put it, Jerusalem "was now the metropolis of all the world's Jews."[4]

In the period before the Great Revolt, then, Eretz Yisrael lived under Roman rule. It was an "occupied" land, with a vassal king (Herod) appointed and controlled by Rome, though "control" may not be the operative word when applied to Herod! But the nature of Roman rule throughout its empire gave a significant amount of autonomy to local populations, particularly around what we today would call "religious" matters. The Romans were not interested in taking over the Temple and imposing their practices and worship on the Jews. The Jews were free to practice their own ways. And of all Jewish practices, none was more understandable to the Romans than the Temple cult with its animal sacrifices, incense, and cast of functionaries— the priests and their retinue. All this "was standard religious behavior for almost everyone in the ancient world."[5] For us today, a religious practice centered around animal sacrifice, libations, and agricultural offerings is so foreign, perhaps even bizarre, that it is hard to fathom. But the spectacle at the pilgrimage festivals must have been an immense spiritual experience for those who attended. Even in our times, anyone who has ever stood in St. Peter's Square on Christmas morning as the pope waves to the crowd or has seen photographs of Mecca at the time of the Haj can get some small sense of what a pilgrimage to the Temple must have meant to the Jews of the first century both within the Land of Israel and in the Diaspora.

And the *idea* of the Temple was equally powerful. This beautiful building that even the Romans admired was truly the appropriate dwelling place for God on earth. The Temple stood for the power and reliability of God himself. To grasp the enormity of what its destruction meant to Akiva and the Jews who lived during his times, we must appreciate how central an institution the Temple was for all of Jewry.

Part of that centrality had to do with the leadership class represented by the priests. This was leadership by lineage, not necessarily by merit. To be a priest a man had to be born into the priestly line. Given the wealth associated with the Temple, alongside the status of the institution, the priests represented a kind of aristocracy among the Jews. Akiva's story is one of a person from a humble background, a kind of counterreality to that of the priests.

There were the beginnings of another institution, the synagogue, while the Temple still stood—though it is not entirely clear what took place in this new setting. Recent scholarship has shown that although synagogues shared certain commonalities, the ancient synagogue was not a single type of institution.[6] They varied in their roles partially depending on geographical location (and here I am speaking only about synagogues in Palestine; synagogues in the Diaspora had a somewhat different function).[7] Some synagogues were likely to have been places for prayer or public reading of the Torah; others were for study; others were more like public buildings used for meetings. Eventually, over the course of many years, synagogues came to embody all three of these functions—prayer, learning, and assembly—under one roof. But in the time of Akiva all this was still evolving.

What did it mean to be a Jew in the years before the destruction of the Temple? Of course the Jews were a *nation*, ruled by a foreign power. In addition, they were a *people* and must have thought of themselves in that way. Hence while many Jews lived in Eretz Yisrael (at the time of the destruction scholars today estimate the population of Palestine to have been around one million, with half of them Jews), a significant Jewish population lived in the Diaspora as well (Egypt, Greece, Italy, etc.), and there was a shared cultural kinship between the Jews in Eretz Yisrael and those in other places in the world. Most Jews, within Palestine or in the Diaspora, seemed to have followed certain practices—for example, abstaining from work on the seventh day, and not eating certain foods, such as pork.

But beyond these specific practices, Jews shared certain ideological commitments as well. The historian Seth Schwartz sums it up succinctly: "If many or most Palestinian Jews had been asked what it was that made them what they were . . . they would likely have answered that it was the worship of their one God, in the one Temple of Jerusalem, in accordance with the laws of Torah."[8] These three core elements of what it meant to be a Jew—God, Temple, and Torah—were all profoundly shaken in the aftermath of the destruction of 70 CE.

I have described the flourishing life of Jerusalem during the early years of the first century: a booming economy, a magnificent Temple, a complicated but mostly bearable occupation under the Romans. Then how did things turn out so badly? Not surprisingly, troubles began with succession issues following the death of Herod in 4 BCE. Although Jerusalem was doing well, the question of leadership was unclear, as Herod's heirs battled among themselves and Rome looked on uneasily. Eventually Rome decided to shift leadership to Romans, and a series of governors (prefects or procurators) were appointed rather than naming a new Jewish king to succeed Herod. Among that list of Roman rulers was, most famously, Pontius Pilate, who ruled from 26 to 36 CE. Pilate, of course, was the Roman governor at the time of the crucifixion of Jesus, but he also made a series of either conscious or unconscious blunders in dealing with the Jewish population in general.

Pilate was not the only problem, just the most well-known to us today. The procurator who sparked the Great Revolt was Gessius Florus, who took over in 64 CE. According to Josephus, Gessius Florus never omitted "any sort of violence, nor any unjust sort of punishment; . . . it was this Florus who necessitated us [the Jews] to take up arms against the Romans, while we thought it better to be destroyed at once, than by little and little" (*Antiquities* 20:254–57).

Thus, to follow Josephus, one explanation for the Great Revolt is that it was a product of bad leadership on the part of the Romans. Where some of the governors could have acted wisely, they instead acted either stupidly or wickedly. But other factors were in play as well. For example, the completion of the Temple meant significant unemployment for all the workers—another fact described as fomenting unhappiness among the Jews.

Schwartz has argued that aside from bad leadership and economic instability, the very nature of the Jews' "exclusivist" culture doomed the relationship of Rome and Jerusalem from birth. The Jewish God and Jewish religious practices could not ever be harmonized with those of Rome. Jews were open to a certain level of integration with Roman mores—knowing Greek or Latin, dressing like a Roman, using Roman courts for certain legal matters—but as Schwartz points out, the Jews were never going to fully conform to what the Romans, as is typical of colonialists in any age, may have viewed as merely "universal."[9]

No matter what the causes, the outcome was disastrous. In the year 70 CE Jerusalem and its Temple were destroyed. Thousands of Jews—hundreds of thousands in all likelihood— were killed, and "a huge percentage of the population was removed from the country, or at the very least, displaced from their homes."[10] The destruction of Jerusalem undermined the ideals of God, Temple, and Torah that were at the heart of Jewish consciousness and raised the deepest questions imaginable for the Jews of Akiva's time: Where was God and what was God's power in the light of the disaster? What is the meaning of worship in a world without the Temple? How can the Torah be understood in the aftermath of tragedy? These were among the most powerful issues that would confront Akiva during his life.

We have looked at the realities that dominated the large-scale picture of Akiva's world—the nature of Roman rule in Palestine, the Temple in its glory followed by the trauma of the Great Revolt and destruction of Jerusalem. Against this backdrop we see the first stirrings of the phenomenon that we have come to call "the rabbis."[11] Of course we know Akiva as *Rabbi* Akiva, but how exactly did "the rabbis" come into existence? About this question historians remain unclear. As Schwartz puts it, "It seems unlikely that the earliest history of the Rabbinic movement can be reconstructed."[12] As with any complex historical phenomenon, pinpointing the origins of the history of the rabbis is not a simple task, particularly given the lack of formal documentation from the time. So we should not be surprised that historians disagree about the nature of how the rabbis first came to be.

Rabbinic literature has a famous statement that describes its origins, the beginning of the Mishnaic tractate Avot ("Fathers" or "Founders"):[13] "Moses received Torah on Sinai and passed it on to Joshua, Joshua to the Elders, the Elders to the Prophets, the Prophets to the Men of the Great Assembly." Who were these "Elders"? It's not clear. Who were the "Men of the Great Assembly"? Indeed, what *was* the Great Assembly? This is also not clear. And how exactly do the "Prophets" fit into this? We don't know. The first two chapters of Avot are not so much a recounting of history as a political argument, an attempt to establish the legitimacy of the rabbis. We begin with Moses, move through Joshua, and soon enough are meeting the Ur-history of rabbinic Judaism—the masters Hillel and Shammai, and others—then on to the early rabbi heroes, Yohanan ben Zakkai and his five students, two of whom were the main teachers of Rabbi Akiva, who himself finally appears in the middle of chapter 2 of Tractate Avot. In other words, the revelation of Torah follows a direct line from God's hand to Moses to the true inheritors of the tradition of Torah, the rabbis. But this is history as told from the point of view of the rabbis themselves. How the rabbis *actually* emerged is a murkier story.[14]

The conventional narrative links the origins of the rabbis to the Pharisees, one of the so-called sects that existed within the Jewish community during the Second Temple period. Josephus—most prominently, but there are other sources as well—speaks about three Jewish sects: the Pharisees, the Sadducees, and the Essenes.[15] The Essenes, a kind of monastic and perhaps apocalyptically oriented group, are often associated with the desert community of Qumran, famous for the Dead Sea Scrolls. The Sadducees were said to be associated with the Temple and the priestly class, and the Pharisees were known for strict adherence to certain religious principles and practices. Unfortunately, the Pharisees have left behind so little material that it is hard to know exactly what they stood for. As the scholar Steven Fraade puts it, "Although the rabbis' most immediate intellectual and spiritual forebears were likely to have been the Pharisees . . . , they have left us no surviving writings of any kind."[16] There certainly seems to be some significant connection between what the Pharisees were and what the rabbis became, but the direct and clear linkage scholars once assumed is now viewed as considerably more nuanced and complex. Indeed, it is interesting to note that "at no point in antiquity did the rabbis clearly see themselves either as Pharisees or as descendants of Pharisees."[17]

Who were the rabbis in their original formation? Most likely, Schwartz suggests, "the battered, drastically reduced remnant of the large pre-Destruction class of legal/religious functionaries, many of whom were probably priests and/or sectarians. To the extent that they began to coalesce into an organization within a few decades of 70, it was more likely from a sense of shared need for mutual support than in the pursuit of some grand . . . scheme to preserve Judaism in the absence of a Temple—an intention often anachronistically ascribed to them by modern scholars."[18] This conception is directly related to the way that current-day scholars have been rethinking the nature and importance of the sects. To us, the word "sect" seems to refer almost to a cult, something out of the mainstream. But does that represent what the early Jewish sects were? Perhaps the sects were more like voluntary associations that one joined. And, most importantly, were the various groups really so different from one another? The trend in scholarship nowadays takes a different stance from the older view of factions in conflict, stressing instead "the strength of the core ideology of Judaism; powerful devotion, which united the sectarians even as disagreement over details of interpretation divided them."[19]

In the concept of the newer historians, then, Jewish life at the time before the destruction of the Temple was not fragmented by sectarianism and was much more unified and centralized than was previously supposed. It was the disaster of 70 CE that threw Jewish life into disarray. And that chaos was not calmed by the rabbis coming to the rescue—at least not for a very long time. Instead, the rabbis started out as a small and self-enclosed group, creating a culture that would eventually blossom into what we now call "rabbinic Judaism." The approach of recent historians is clearly and succinctly summarized by the Talmud scholar Beth Berkowitz. Following the destruction wrought by the Great Revolt,

> the Sages coalesced among the shards. While historians disagree about a variety of issues ... at the same time, they share a vision of these Sages. ... (the earliest Rabbis dating to the late first century and second century), as a small, informally organized group struggling for authority in a political structure in which their exercise of power depended solely on persuasion. The Sages were an exclusive and separatist clan, ambivalent about their relationship to the majority of more acculturated Jews, who were in turn ambivalent toward but most often simply ignorant of the small group of Rabbis living, legislating, and studying in their largely Greco-Roman paganized midst. ... The power of the Rabbis as we know it from the medieval period ... is no longer taken for granted in the Tannaitic era, which is newly conceived as an intensely formative period in the development of the Rabbis. Rather than an institutionalized religious hegemony who rallied the Jewish community around their interpretive authority, the Rabbis were much more likely to have been an embattled, almost invisible sect within second-century Judaism.[20]

Berkowitz describes the world in which Akiva lived his life. He was part—indeed a crucially central part—of that "small, informally organized group" aiming to envision a relationship to Torah in the light of the tragedy that had struck the community. Perhaps the power of "persuasion" is precisely what Akiva offered with his creative interpretative genius.

Having explored in brief the complicated story of the *origins* of that group of individuals we call "the rabbis," what might we surmise about them? Who were they, and what characterized their world? When we hear the term "rabbi" today it brings to mind a number of different and related images. These have been fashioned by our own experiences, our reading and representations of rabbis in popular culture. First and foremost, we associate rabbis with synagogues, although today there certainly are rabbis who are employed in other arenas. Still, although not every rabbi works in a synagogue, very few synagogues don't have a rabbi. Within the world of the synagogue (broadly defined) rabbis perform or lead important rituals (marriage, burial, naming of babies) for their congregants' life events. Second, we think of rabbis—like doctors or lawyers—as professionals who have received a structured and *formal* kind of training. They have sat in classes and taken examinations or written papers to "graduate" with rabbinic ordination. They may have studied in a liberal seminary or an Orthodox yeshiva, but they have been through a course of study determined by standards and traditions.

Third, we think of rabbis as spiritual and intellectual leaders of the Jewish community. They have attained *status* through their role and through their achievements. Fourth, rabbis provide pastoral care—they counsel couples before or during marriage, visit the sick, and look after their communities in a variety of ways. Finally, in some sectors of the Jewish community—generally, the Orthodox world, but this applies to the liberal Jewish community as well—rabbis are judges: they help adjudicate matters of religious practice or civil disputes using the framework of Jewish law and precedent.

Although these elements are all very familiar to us today, virtually none of them obtained in Akiva's world.[21] To begin with, let us get a sense of numbers. By reading rabbinic literature one might feel that there were enormous numbers of rabbis, but in fact the count is actually rather small. The reader of rabbinic texts may imagine a larger number simply because these sources—particularly the Babylonian Talmud—will place side by side on the same page rabbis who lived at very different times (and places). The generational count is obscured by merging *all* the rabbis across hundreds of years into one large pool. But a simple exercise of looking at the specific rabbis who appear in the Mishnah reveals a grand total of fifty-four who lived more or less at the same time as Akiva.[22] Of course this is only a rough method: there may well have been rabbis whose words were simply not recorded by the Mishnah, for example. But even by this unsophisticated method it is clear that we are talking about a tiny population.

Thus the rabbis during this early period were a small and insulated group, found more in towns and villages than in cities.[23] They were not interested in spreading their teachings to the masses; in fact, they looked down on the masses, as we can see from numerous rabbinic statements about other Jews who wasted their time in foolish pursuits rather than studying Torah. Much of that disregard may have emanated from the fact that by and large scholars have argued that the early rabbis came from the wealthy tier of Palestinian Jewish society, or at least those one notch down from the top.[24] This perspective differs markedly from the older view of scholars who identified the earliest rabbis as "plebeians" (to use Louis Finkelstein's term).[25] Indeed, the humble origin of Akiva is all the more remarkable given the rabbinic world that he entered.

More importantly, the rabbis did not create the institutions—such as schools for Torah learning—that one would expect from a group interested in spreading its teachings. As the historian Shaye Cohen has put it: "They had little inclination and availed themselves of few opportunities to propagate their way of life among the masses. Their judicial authority extended to a few circumscribed topics only. The rabbis were but a small part of Jewish society, an insular group which produced an insular literature."[26] One of the oddities here is that the rabbis of Akiva's time believed in an ideology that required Torah study as obligatory on all, but they did not create an infrastructure to allow this to happen.

What was the environment in which the rabbis' own Torah study took place? Rabbinic literature uses a number of different terms for the place in which rabbinic discussions and debates occurred—the two most well-known being the Beit Midrash (literally "house of study") and yeshiva (literally "sitting place"— the rabbinic academy). Traditional scholarship always viewed the Beit Midrash or the yeshiva as a formal institution, much as we would view a school today. Namely, in that standard view, it was led by a rabbi or rabbis; it had a kind of formal curriculum; and the "students" more or less "enrolled" and in many cases were themselves "ordained" as rabbis after their course of study.

Recent scholarship has raised significant questions about these assumptions. In a path-breaking book some years ago the historian David Goodblatt investigated the sources about the settings for Jewish learning in Babylonia during the Sasanian Empire (the Sasanid dynasty ruled Babylonia from the early third century CE until the mid-seventh century, essentially the same time period of the Babylonian Talmud). He concluded that large stable academies (yeshivot) came into existence only at a considerably later period and that the Babylonian Jewish community was characterized by what Goodblatt calls "disciple circles." A disciple circle was not a school. A school, Goodblatt writes, has "a staff, a curriculum, and most important, a life of its own, a corporate identity. Students come and go, teachers leave and are replaced, the head of the school dies and a new one is appointed—the institution goes on. A disciple circle, on the other hand, does not transcend its principals. Disciples meet with a master and study with him. . . . When the master dies, the disciple circle disbands. . . . What I have in mind is a relationship similar to that of a group of apprentices and a master craftsman."[27] Later rabbinic sources, which give us the image of a formal institution much like a school, are only projecting back into the past the world of these later sources, viewing the past through the lens of the present, in the manner of a sixteenth- or seventeenth-century Dutch painting of a biblical scene that has windmills in the background.

In Goodblatt's view, the "academy" is a posttalmudic phenomenon. Instead he sees disciple circles that met informally; though there might have been a special building in which the disciple circle met, more often than not we should imagine these discussions taking place in the home of a master or of a wealthy individual who gave the teacher space for his classes. Goodblatt's theory—with some modifications—has by and large stood the test of time.

But what the research on the study hall in Babylonia leaves unclear is what the Beit Midrash may have looked like years before, in *Palestine*, during Akiva's time. Were there formal institutions of learning, as suggested in some of the stories about Akiva, or were these also anachronistic framings by the later edited talmudic sources, the "fictive retrojection of institutions back into a formative age"?[28] The historian Catherine Hezser comes to a conclusion about Palestine similar to Goodblatt's view of Babylonia: "Study houses in Roman Palestine seem to have been (rooms in) private houses or apartments or public buildings where people customarily met to study Torah. . . . There is no reason to assume that study houses, houses of meeting, or halls were 'rabbinic academies.' . . . Those study houses which were associated with a particular rabbi would have ceased to exist with that rabbi's death. . . . Study houses do not seem to have been particularly organized at all."[29]

Given the rabbis' insularity, it should not be surprising to us that rabbis in the first and second centuries were not what today we would call communal leaders; the association of "rabbi" and "synagogue" that seems so obvious to us today did not develop until many years after Akiva's death, perhaps beginning only in the third century of the Common Era and evolving slowly over time. It would not have occurred to Akiva that his role as rabbi should have anything to do with a synagogue. More surprising, as Shaye Cohen shows, rabbis did not seem to have a particularly important role as judges.[30] Examination of the literature before 200 CE suggests that rabbinic judges saw only a small number of cases, and most of those dealt with fairly obscure issues, such as matters of ritual purity. They had little to do with civil cases and surprisingly little to do with matters about which we might have expected them to provide leadership—such as observing the Sabbath and eating kosher foods.

The beginnings of the change in the role of rabbis in the direction of what seems more natural to us today are usually attributed to the influence of Rabbi Judah the Patriarch (often translated as Judah the Prince), who lived a few generations after Rabbi Akiva. In fact a rabbinic tradition in the Talmud reports that he was born on the day that Akiva died. If not historically accurate, this tradition certainly expresses the talmudic notion of a chain of great leadership—an idea that one often sees in rabbinic literature. Rabbi Judah expanded the reach of the rabbis into cities, in tune with the greater urbanization of Palestine. Tzipori (Sepphoris), Lod (Lydda), Tiberias, and other cities became centers for Jewish study. He found ways to take a wider range of social classes into the rabbinic group, and he had the full support of the Roman authorities so that rabbis actually came to be seen as leaders of their communities.[31] But all this developed years after the life of Akiva. In Akiva's time it is fair to say that there was no "rabbinic movement" as we might have supposed. Hezser captures what is likely to have been the reality of the time: "The rabbinic movement may best be described as an informal network of relationships which constituted a personal alliance system. Rabbis seem to have maintained intimate friendship ties with small circles of colleagues whom they met on various informal occasions. They seem to have visited their rabbinic friends at home, shared their meals with them, attended their family ceremonies, and traveled with them to baths and markets. Discussion of Torah may have taken place at any of these social occasions."[32] In essence, then, for Akiva and his colleagues, "the rabbis" were simply a small circle of friends. The "movement" was to develop later and over the centuries, but its beginnings can be seen in the lives of Akiva and his colleagues. With this background in mind we now turn to the stories about Akiva's origins.

2

A Self-Created Sage

As I HAVE DISCUSSED, it is impossible to reconstruct the "true" biography of Rabbi Akiva, given the distance in time and the nature of the sources available to us. Instead, we are *imagining* a biography of Akiva. But even here our task is complicated by the fact that we are presented with a variety of sources about Akiva from a variety of places within the vast corpus of rabbinic literature. These sources differ from one another—sometimes considerably and sometimes in only small details—raising the question of how we should deal with these differences in constructing the story of his life.

Texts from the earliest layer of the rabbinic world were reshaped and adapted by later authorities, sometimes because of inherent complications involved in transmitting oral traditions and sometimes (at least we suppose) for polemical or apologetic reasons. In looking at the stories of the life of Rabbi Akiva—particularly those about his beginnings and his marriage—these difficulties become particularly obvious. Was Akiva an unmarried shepherd who began his studies of Torah for the love of a good woman? Or was he already a married man with a young son when, through his own intuition, he discovered the importance of learning? Both traditions can be found in rabbinic literature.

One conventional approach has been to "harmonize" the various strands, ignoring as best as possible these contradictions and creating a seamless narrative. We can see this tactic in a number of retellings of Akiva's life. On the other side, academic scholars tend to aim at disentangling the various strands of tradition, trying to speculate about the historical processes involved in transmission. Some scholars have focused on looking for the so-called historical kernel (that is, the "real events") embedded within the legend. But, as I have discussed, in recent years the attraction and legitimacy of such an approach has faded for a host of good reasons.[1]

In this chapter I take a different slant. My goal is not to harmonize the various traditions, nor is it to take the academic scholars' approach, though there will be times that I present their insights. Rather, I aim to look at a variety of traditions and hold them up against one another to see what we might imagine about Akiva's early life and why the Jewish tradition has chosen to preserve these tales across the generations. What, in other words, are we meant to learn from exploring the stories about the origin of one of the great heroes of rabbinic culture?

It is worth remembering that the stories and teachings of Akiva are those that have come down to us *after* and *in the light of* the work done by the ancient, anonymous editors of the Talmud and other rabbinic works. We are heirs to that *entire* tradition, and focusing on the complex multilayered biography of Akiva with all its contradictions seems to be the wisest course—that and maintaining a self-consciousness about our efforts in which we keep in mind the usefulness of acknowledging the ways that historical processes of editing and transmission are valuable interpretive tools. This point of view has something in common with the approach of contemporary biblical scholars: yes, we recognize that the Bible is composed of a set of complex, interwoven sources, and at times it is helpful as scholars and interpreters to pull those pieces apart and look at them individually; but in the end, the Bible as we have it *now*, as it has been known for centuries, has its own integrity.

These matters are particularly relevant when we turn to the early life of Rabbi Akiva. Here we notice that in fact there are two main traditions about his origins: one we might call the philosophical version, and the other, the romantic version. In this chapter I explore the philosophical version; I look at the romantic tale in chapter 3. The philosophical telling of the story is found in a rabbinic text known as Avot de Rabbi Natan ("The Fathers According to Rabbi Nathan"). Avot de Rabbi Natan is a text with a complicated history: parts of it are quite old, dating back close to the time of Akiva himself, but scholars have now shown that other sections can be dated to as late as the early Middle Ages.[2] Avot de Rabbi Natan has a good deal in common with Tractate Avot, which in a slightly expanded version is more popularly known as Pirkei Avot (literally "Chapters of the Fathers" though it is often translated as "Ethics of the Fathers").

Avot differs from almost anything else in the rabbinic library because it involves virtually none of what most characterizes the literature of rabbis—that is, disputation around matters of law and interpretation of Torah verses. Nor does it contain legends about biblical or rabbinic figures. Instead, it consists of a series of fairly pithy statements about life and ethical behavior. It is eminently quotable: very few people have sat through sermons of contemporary rabbis without hearing quotations from Pirkei Avot.

Avot de Rabbi Natan has much in common with the Mishnaic tractate Avot, but it does contain legends about the rabbis that we do not find in the Mishnah, most importantly a story about Akiva's early life. Making things a bit more complicated is the fact that Avot de Rabbi Natan exists in two versions, called, without much originality, Version A and Version B. We need not go into more detail about the comparison of these two versions; suffice it to say that the story of the origins of Rabbi Akiva appears in both versions of Avot de Rabbi Natan with some small modifications, which I will point out. Here is the rendition from Version A:

> What was the beginning of Rabbi Akiva? It is said: He was forty years old and he had not studied anything. One time he stood at the mouth of a well and said: "Who hollowed out this stone?" He was told: "It is the water which falls upon it every day, continually." They said to him: "Akiva, have you not read the verse, 'water wears away stone'?" (Job 14:19). Immediately Rabbi Akiva drew the inference that the verse applied to himself: "if what is soft wears down the hard, how much the more so shall the words of the Torah, which are as hard as iron, hollow out my heart, which is flesh and blood!" Immediately he turned to the study of Torah.
>
> He went together with his son and they appeared before a teacher of young children. Said Rabbi Akiva to him: "Master, teach me Torah." Rabbi Akiva took one end of the tablet and his son the other end of the tablet. The teacher wrote down "aleph bet" and he learned it; "aleph tav," and he learned it; the book of Leviticus, and he learned it. He went on studying until he learned the entire Torah.
>
> Avot de Rabbi Natan, Version A, chapter 6[3]

The story in Version B is quite similar to this one though with some interesting differences. Both are based around the same verse from Job and the insight that Akiva gains by looking at a phenomenon in the physical world. In Version B we learn of a specific location for the story (Lod in Hebrew, Lydda in

English—a city about ten miles southeast of modern Tel Aviv), and instead of a well created by water, Akiva sees a trench next to a well that has been dug out by a rope being dragged through the dirt.

Version B adds a nice touch in which the anonymous "they" of our story ask Akiva, "Why are you so surprised?" before quoting the verse from Job. In addition, Version B fleshes out the curriculum that Akiva learns. In Version B he learns not only the Hebrew alphabet ("aleph bet" begins the Hebrew alphabet; "tav" ends it—in other words he learned the entire alphabet from first to last) and then the book of Leviticus, the traditional starting place for biblical study, but also "scripture, Targum, midrash, halakhah, aggadah, arcane speech, and parables. He learned everything!" (Targum is the ancient translation of the Torah into the vernacular language of the times, Aramaic. And as we have seen, midrash is the general term for rabbinic interpretive understandings of the Bible; *halakhah* is Jewish law, and *aggadah* is, loosely speaking, Jewish legend.)[4]

Let us turn back to the story as told in Version A, keeping in mind these small variations. It begins by asking what was the "beginning" of Rabbi Akiva. The answer—certainly to a modern reader—is rather surprising. We do not, as we might expect, hear of his birth, his parentage, his ancestry, his geographical location. In other words, we learn nothing in the mode of "biography" as we today might understand it. He appears as if out of nowhere; he is from no place, and he has no background. The text begins with a forty-year-old man who had not studied Torah. That is all we know. Perhaps we are meant to emphasize the word "rabbi" here: What was the beginning of *Rabbi* Akiva— that is, what led him to become a rabbi?

What we are given is the picture of a self-created individual. Akiva is someplace out in nature (near Lod, as Version B tells us?). He is not alone; other unnamed people are nearby, and for some unexplained reason Akiva begins to think about the well that he sees near him. This is not, it is clear, a well built by humans but is something formed by nature. He asks the people around him, Who made this well? They respond, perhaps somewhat oddly to us, not with a "scientific" answer but with a quotation from scripture. They tell him that the water has worn away the rock,[5] but the real proof is the quotation from Job.

"Why are you so surprised, Akiva?" they are saying to him, "haven't you read the verse from Job that tells us that water wears away stone?" Who are these scripture-quoting compatriots of Akiva's? The text doesn't tell us. The assumption seems to be that *anyone* should know such verses and anyone should know that the way to understand the natural world is through the lens of scripture. But of course Akiva knows nothing. He doesn't know Job; he has no knowledge of Torah at all. We the readers have been told this from the opening of the story: he was forty years old, and he had not studied anything.

To associate knowledge of the world and how it works (the way the well is formed) with knowledge of Torah is to suggest that the key to understanding *anything* is through Torah. And perhaps that is what Version B means to tell us when it says "he learned everything." Through learning Torah Akiva becomes a philosopher, in the old sense of the word—one who knows the totality of things. For Akiva this becomes a major theme of his life—plumbing the depths of Torah in all its intricacies and with all the imagination and creativity that a person can bring to that task.

But the point of the story here is to communicate something more than the idea that in order to understand the natural world, one must study Torah. The more dominant motif of our story is the great *personal* insight Akiva acquires as he watches water cutting through stone. If water can cut through stone, he thinks, my heart can also be softened. And as we read the story, we are taken by surprise—because Akiva's question, "Who hollowed out this stone?" leads us to expect a different answer. At first this seems more like a *theological* question, a question about God and creation that would lead to Akiva's discovery of divine mastery of all of nature, and we expect an answer to go in that direction.[6]

But Akiva seems be asking a question about himself, not a theological one: what will it take to hollow out *my* heart? Judah Goldin, a scholar who published the standard translation of Version A in 1955, chose "hollow out" to translate the Hebrew word in the original text (*hakak*), though I think that "carve out" or "shape" is probably closer to what the text means here— the Hebrew word has a number of closely related meanings. It appears that he is saying that his hard heart needs to be softened, or shaped the way a chisel shapes stone.

Much here is puzzling: Why does Akiva think that his heart needs softening or shaping? What does it mean to have one's heart changed in that way? Why is Torah seen to be as hard as iron? It is an uncommon metaphor for Torah in rabbinic literature (unlike, say, Torah as a tree of life). In fact, it appears in only one source that I could find—a fairly well-known midrash that compares the words of Torah to well-planted iron nails— but that source seems to be much more about Torah's constancy than its power to break or shape the heart.[7]

"Hardening of the heart" is a biblical motif, most familiar to us from the story of Pharaoh and the Exodus from Egypt. In the Exodus story it is pretty clear that the meaning of a hardened heart is related to stubbornness or a lack of compassion on the part of Pharaoh. The same Hebrew word appears in a different way in Psalm 95:8, "Harden not your heart," where the meaning of a hardened heart in the context of the psalm is less about stubbornness or cruelty as it was in the case of Pharaoh than it is a theological matter—not trusting in God.

In our story the insight Akiva has about water wearing away stone is applied to his own heart. Torah, he sees, might come to "hollow out" or "shape" his hardened heart. The two different meanings of hardening the heart from the biblical context may both apply here. Perhaps, we are meant to understand, Akiva is commenting on a lack of personal religious faith. As if reading the message in Psalm 95, Akiva now understands that he is distant from God. What he believes that Torah will give him is a chance to connect with that which is transcendent; and, at the same time, he sees himself like the biblical Pharaoh, locked in stubbornness and lacking compassion. These two dimensions about the purposes of learning Torah, the theological and the personal (or ethical), are themes that we will see throughout Akiva's life. The origin story, in other words, prefigures the enterprise of the rest of his life as the traditional sources have presented it to us.

One peculiarity that might strike the reader in this interpretation is the notion that Akiva was lacking a compassionate heart. Where might we see this element of his character? Of course we know very little from these stories about his early life. Indeed from the point of view of the story we are looking at here his life begins at age forty. But Akiva makes a few remarks in other places in which he looks back on his youth. One of the strangest is a comment quoted in the Talmud:

> When I was an *am ha-aretz* I said, "Who will give me a sage so that I could bite him like a donkey?" His students said to him: "Rabbi, you mean bite him like a dog." He replied to them: "No, a donkey. Because a donkey bites and breaks bones; the dog bites but doesn't break a bone!"
>
> b. Pesahim "Passover" 49b

The context of this odd recollection is a number of statements in the Talmud about the relationship between the sages and the *am ha-aretz* (plural *amei ha-aretz*), a term for the unlearned masses who care little about their religious obligations.[8]

This is a strikingly vicious statement by Akiva, and one

cannot help but feel that he is reflecting back on his early life with the anger and regret with which a reformed sinner will recall his early misdeeds. It is not a psychologically surprising phenomenon. But the added dimension here is that it provides an additional way of thinking about his quest to "unharden" his heart. The ethical shortcomings of Akiva's early life, the aspects of himself that he feels he needs to change as he stands by the well, may be reflected in this story of his antipathy toward the very figures in society—the rabbis—with whom he would eventually identify.

Viewed from the standpoint of historical scholarship today, making the connection between the story at the well and Akiva's comments about being an *am ha-aretz* is not so simple. The source for the donkey comment is the Babylonian Talmud, a work that was put together some four hundred years after Akiva's time. As we saw in the last chapter, scholars have noted that the view of the rabbis living in the Land of Israel toward the *amei ha-aretz* is essentially one of distance or uninterest. But the Babylonian perspective was considerably harsher, owing perhaps to the differences between the general culture in Palestine (Roman) and the dominant culture in Babylonia (Persian), an interpretation suggested by the Talmud scholar Richard Kalmin more than fifteen years ago.[9]

The attitude toward the *amei ha-aretz* went far beyond uninterest or disdain in Babylonia, as evidenced by the statement of Akiva and by other similarly nasty comments that appear on the same page of the Talmud. As scholars have looked at the sources known to date from an earlier period—closer to the years during which Akiva lived—we don't have as much evidence for the kind of extreme antipathy between the common folk and scholars as reported in the talmudic passage about the donkey and the dog. Hence it makes sense to view the story as an interpolation from the later traditions in the Babylonian Talmud. But it does provide an insight into how the talmudic rabbis wanted us to view Akiva's early years: he was hostile, and then, essentially, he "converted" to the ways of the rabbis.

The second part of the story of Akiva at the well highlights another central theme of Akiva's life: his intellectual brilliance. And indeed the notion of his beginning his studies at the age of forty serves the purpose of emphasizing his natural gifts even more than if he had started learning at a young age. That is, we are being told: he began study so late, yet look how much he attained! It is, of course, tempting to read this story as promulgating Akiva as an example of the idea that anyone can begin learning at any age. And so teachers and parents have used it throughout Jewish history, to be sure.

Yet the more dominant theme may be the opposite: look at the genius of this extraordinary man. He began with nothing and became the greatest Torah sage of his time. Only a person of immense talent could have achieved so much.

Interestingly there is a hint of Akiva's natural-born talent even before we get to the second part of our story where we see him beginning with aleph-bet and eventually mastering "everything." Akiva is standing by the well that has been created by the action of water wearing away stone. He has heard the verse from Job quoted to him and then we read: "Immediately Rabbi Akiva drew the inference that the verse applied to himself." There is a subtle point that the Hebrew language expresses to the reader. Translated here as "drew the inference," the text *literally* says, "Immediately Akiva applied the principle of *kal vahomer*" and saw that the water wearing away rock would be analogous to his own situation.

Akiva has certainly "drawn an inference" from the water and the rock, but it is an inference of a particular sort. The phrase *kal vahomer* is a technical term in rabbinic rhetoric for a certain type of argumentation. The term is often best translated as "how much the more so." The structure of the logic is as follows: if X is true in a lesser situation, then *kal vahomer* (how much the more so) should *X* be true in a greater situation. If we are supposed to get a good night's sleep every night, *kal vahomer* (how much the more so), should we get a good night's sleep when we are taking an important exam on the next day. If a forty-year-old would be wise to have a flu shot, *kal vahomer* (how much the more so), should an eighty-year-old get that injection. Akiva's brilliance as a student (which we see in the second part of the story) is hinted at in his "discovering" the classic rabbinic principle of *kal vahomer* on his own with no training at all in rabbinic logic. It is as if to say that Akiva already has within him the seeds of rabbinic scholarship. He is a sage waiting to happen.

The story told in Avot de Rabbi Natan does not end with Akiva in the schoolhouse. As we saw earlier, he sat with his son and began with the aleph-bet and kept on studying until he had learned "the entire Torah," or as Version B has it, until "he learned everything." But the story continues with Akiva now turning to two of the greatest Torah scholars of his time:

> He went and sat before Rabbi Eliezer and Rabbi Joshua. "My masters," he said to them, "uncover the meaning of Mishnah for me."
>
> When they told him one law, he went and sat by himself. "This aleph," he thought, "why was it written? This bet, why was it written? This thing, why was it said?" He came back and asked them—and reduced them to silence.
>
> Avot de Rabbi Natan, Version A, chapter 6

It is interesting to note that all this happens *after* Akiva has learned "everything" virtually on his own. (An unnamed teacher is mentioned in the first part of the story, but the fact that the person is anonymous suggests that Akiva was not studying with one of the early and well-known rabbinic masters.) Only after this period of individual study does he turn to higher authorities, Rabbi Eliezer ben Hyrcanus and Rabbi Joshua ben Hananiah. He asks them to teach him Mishnah; possibly this is an anachronism. Mishnah, the great compilation of Rabbi Judah the Patriarch that forms the cornerstone of much of later rabbinic literature, was not edited until a hundred years after Akiva's death. But perhaps the text does not mean to refer to *the* Mishnah but rather "Mishnah" in the sense of "a teaching." The distinction is not terribly significant in this case—as I've said before, these texts about Akiva are put together much later than the period during which the action is supposed to have taken place, and the editors do not seem overly concerned about historical precision, a value much more of our time than of theirs.

He is learning Jewish law, or *halakhah*. He has gone to study with these two great teachers, but the curious thing about the story is, what exactly are Rabbi Eliezer and Rabbi Joshua teaching *him* anyway? In fact, it seems that Akiva is the one teaching *them*, or at any rate, he is the one confounding them. They tell him one *halakhah*, and he goes off by himself and returns with questions that they cannot answer. Akiva is consistently portrayed throughout these stories as a self-made man. What he possesses, it appears, is the ability to penetrate the tradition by asking the most fundamental questions of "why." He ponders each letter in every word with a question, and then he ponders the sense of the whole ("this thing, why was it said?") as well. Surely, Eliezer and Joshua have thought about these matters before, but there must be something in the way that Akiva thinks about them that is beyond their grasp.

The story continues with a kind of commentary on Akiva and his relationship with his teachers:

> Rabbi Shimon ben Eleazar says: "I will tell you a parable to explain what this matter is like. It was like a stonecutter who was cutting away in the mountains. Once he took his axe and sat on the side of a mountain and began chipping away tiny stones. People came by and asked him: 'What are you doing?'

He said to them: 'Look, I am uprooting this mountain and throwing it into the Jordan River.'

"They said to him: 'You can't uproot an entire mountain!'

"But he continued chipping away at the mountain until he came to a large rock. He crawled under it, broke it, uprooted it, and flung it into the Jordan, saying to it: 'This is not your place—that is!'

"This is what Rabbi Akiva did to Rabbi Eliezer and Rabbi Joshua."

Rabbi Tarfon said: "Akiva, about you scripture says, 'He dams up the sources of the streams so that hidden things may be brought to light' (Job 28:11). Things concealed from human beings, Rabbi Akiva brought to light."

Avot de Rabbi Natan, Version A, chapter 6

Most rabbinic texts engage with biblical verses in some manner or another, so it is not unusual—as we saw with Akiva at the well—that the text gives a central role to the quotation from the Bible. It is often instructive to look at the larger biblical context when the rabbis quote a verse since the single verse mentioned may be intended to allude to other verses within the same biblical section. Indeed, if we look at the context in Job of the verse quoted here (28:11) we see that the previous verses increase the connection to the parable of the stonecutter. And Avot de Rabbi Natan Version B, in telling a similar version of this parable, brings in all three of the relevant verses:

Man sets his hand against the flinty rock
And overturns mountains by the roots.

He carves out channels through rock;
His eyes behold every precious thing.

He dams up the sources of the streams
So that hidden things may be brought to light.

Job 28:9–11

It's interesting that the metaphoric core with which we began—hardness and softness, water and rock—returns here, though no longer focused on softening the hardened heart. Instead, the poem from the book of Job is interpreted by Rabbi Tarfon as a commentary on Akiva's ability to penetrate the difficulties of the Torah. The Torah—which Akiva described as hard as iron at the scene by the well—is now viewed as hard as rock. As the parable is explained, Akiva is like the stonecutter who is able to carve through that rock; more than that, he can stop the powerful flow of water. But the *purpose* of those actions is shown as well: he uncovers secrets; he sees what others cannot see: "every precious thing" beneath those rocks and "hidden things" beneath the flow of water.

Rabbi Shimon ben Eleazar uses the parable of the stonecutter to describe Akiva as the student of Rabbi Eliezer and Rabbi Joshua, and Shimon's description of Akiva's effect is stark and cutting: "This is what Rabbi Akiva *did to* Rabbi Eliezer and Rabbi Joshua." We are brought up short by the bluntness of the comment, but if we look back at the description of their interchanges, perhaps it is not so surprising. Akiva asks questions that take them aback.

We can view the parable of the stonecutter in two related ways. First, it is precisely the way Rabbi Shimon describes it: the rocks, the mountains of understanding that Eliezer and Joshua had acquired, are now smashed into pieces. They are overturned, thrown into the Jordan, as it were.

And it also appears that the story is meant to tell us something else: part of what we are being shown is Akiva's invention of a whole new *method* of rabbinic discourse. That method is one of the things that characterizes his entire career: the close and detailed interrogation of Torah, interpretation at its deepest and, we might say, at its most *optimistic* core. I say optimistic to mean that Akiva has a fundamental faith in the unending richness of the Torah, of the ability of Torah to yield more and more levels of interpretation. Of course from a scholar's perspective, Akiva is not the inventor of this approach to interpretation. A long history precedes him, and an even longer expanse comes after his time. But in the eyes of this particular story, he is the creator of something revolutionary. He becomes the hero of a new way of reading Torah.

In the story about Akiva from Avot de Rabbi Natan we know nothing about the reaction of Rabbi Eliezer and Rabbi Joshua to Akiva's questions except that they are reduced to silence. It is the parable of the stonecutter by Shimon ben Eleazar and his curt remark about Eliezer and Joshua ("This is what Rabbi Akiva did to Rabbi Eliezer and Rabbi Joshua") that gives the reader the interpretation of the story.

Later in this book we will look in some detail at the nature of Akiva's relationship with his rabbinic teachers and colleagues, but it is worth pausing here to consider Rabbi Eliezer ben Hyrcanus as he appears in Avot de Rabbi Natan. Eliezer is often identified as one of Akiva's teachers (along with Rabbi Joshua ben Hananiah and Rabban Gamaliel II), but it is hard to see that Akiva learns anything from him at all. As we will later see, Akiva and Eliezer have a long and somewhat tragic history together, and one wonders: Are the seeds of later contention sown here in the Version A telling of Akiva's experience as Eliezer's student? The question is particularly relevant because the story of the origins of Rabbi Akiva in Avot de Rabbi Natan is directly followed by the story of the origins of Rabbi Eliezer, as if we are meant to view these two rabbis as parallel figures.

Eliezer's story begins like this:

> What was the beginning of Rabbi Eliezer ben Hyrcanus? He was twenty-two years old and had not yet studied Torah. Once he decided: "I will go and study Torah with Rabban Yohanan ben Zakkai." His father Hyrcanus said to him, "You

will not have a taste of food until you have plowed the entire furrow."

Avot de Rabbi Natan, Version A, chapter 6

Like Akiva, Eliezer comes late to the study of Torah, and like Akiva he begins to feel a burning desire to learn. It is possible that Akiva and Eliezer might come to feel a kinship with one another, given their origins, but the differences between the two stories of origin are as significant as their similarities. Akiva, as we have seen, is a man without a past. We know nothing of his parents. Eliezer, on the other hand, has a father, and though the geographical setting is not named, his father appears to be a farmer or landowner; it makes sense to assume that Eliezer has grown up on that farm. Hyrcanus is a boorish man—a fact confirmed by events that occur later in the story—who cannot see the value of Torah and any reason for encouraging his son along that path.

Hyrcanus is certainly insensitive to his son's needs and interests, but Eliezer's desire to learn is so great that he runs away from home, refusing all food until he arrives at Jerusalem to meet the greatest Torah teacher of his time, Rabban Yohanan ben Zakkai. We continue the story from where it left off:

> . . . Eliezer went and appeared before Rabban Yohanan ben Zakkai—until a bad breath rose from Eliezer's mouth. Yohanan ben Zakkai said to him: "Eliezer, my son, have you eaten at all today?"
>
> Silence.
>
> Rabban Yohanan ben Zakkai asked him again.
>
> Again silence.
>
> Rabban Yohanan ben Zakkai sent for the owners of the inn where Eliezer was staying and asked them: "Did Eliezer have anything to eat in your place?"
>
> They replied: "We thought that he was very likely eating with you, master."

He said to them: "And I thought he was very likely eating with you. Between both of us we left Rabbi Eliezer to perish!"

Rabban Yohanan turned to Eliezer and said to him: "Even as a bad breath rose from your mouth, so shall your fame travel because of your mastery of Torah."

Most readers of this story are struck and puzzled by the detail about Eliezer's bad breath, but I think the point here is both practical and metaphoric. In the practical sense, all of us know that a day without eating food will result in bad breath, thanks to the body's natural processes. But metaphorically speaking, Eliezer has chosen not to eat because he is seeking "real" food—namely, Torah. And he is escaping from the father who can't understand his needs even when Eliezer says them out loud. What he discovers is his "true" father—Yohanan ben Zakkai, who can discern what is in Eliezer's heart even when Eliezer remains silent. And the bad breath gives the story a chance to give the punch line to Yohanan: "Even as a bad breath rose from your mouth, so shall your fame travel because of your mastery of Torah." It is, in other words, a story of a person's transformation—from being unlearned to becoming a scholar—as the breath turns from bad to sweet. The structure of the story is as beautifully honed as a well-formed literary piece.

When we compare Eliezer's story of origin with Akiva's, we see some obvious differences. Akiva comes from nowhere; he is not rebelling against a father—there is no father at all in the tale. There is no backstory in Avot de Rabbi Natan. Akiva simply appears. In the same way, unlike Eliezer, Akiva is not seeking a father substitute. Read psychologically, Akiva's challenge to Rabbi Eliezer and Rabbi Joshua is the unembarrassed attack of an unencumbered man on his elders. Eliezer, on the other hand, needs to respect Yohanan; he needs to turn himself into the son and the disciple. Akiva is a tougher character. He is unhesitant in his challenge to those in authority, and in challenging them, he upends mountains and forges a new path.

In the coda to the Eliezer story, Hyrcanus comes to Jerusalem intent on disinheriting his son. When Rabban Yohanan sees
Hyrcanus enter the room, Yohanan "turns his eyes to Eliezer
and tells him 'You begin and deliver the teaching.' Eliezer replies: 'I cannot even begin.'" He is at a loss for words. Here
once again, the motif of silence returns.

But the story doesn't end there. It continues: "Yohanan
pressed him and the other students pressed him and finally
Eliezer stood and delivered a teaching about things that no
ear had ever heard." As he hears Eliezer's talk, Rabban Yohanan
rises to his feet, kisses Eliezer on the head, and says to him,
"Rabbi Eliezer, my teacher, from you have I learned truth."

It is a sensational and deeply moving ending to the Eliezer
story. The master (Yohanan) has now become the student.
Eliezer has become "Rabbi" Eliezer. The story ennobles
Eliezer but also shows the clear contrast with Akiva. Akiva is
not a man of silence. When Yohanan speaks to Eliezer, the
youthful Eliezer remains silent. When Akiva challenges Eliezer
and Joshua, *they* are silenced. Eliezer is passive. He comes to
Yohanan to absorb learning, and only after doing that, learning
as a disciple, is he able to create his own brand of Torah—"a
teaching about things that no ear had ever heard," as the text
says. But Akiva is self-invented. He has teachers but seems
mostly to be teaching himself. It is not surprising, in this context, that there are places in rabbinic literature in which Akiva
is compared to Moses. We see, for example, this remarkable
statement in Pesikta Rabbati, a midrashic text organized around
the biblical readings for the Jewish festivals and other special
occasions:

> R. Aha said: Things which had not been revealed even to
> Moses were revealed to Rabbi Akiva. To Akiva we can apply
> the verse, "His eyes behold every precious thing" (Job 28:10).
>
> Pesikta Rabbati 14:13

Once again, the same verse from Job that is associated with Akiva in Avot de Rabbi Natan is applied here. Akiva sees what others cannot. Moses is the ultimate prophet in Jewish tradition. His wisdom comes directly from divine revelation. To Rav Aha in this text something about Akiva seems to be at the level of the prophet. It is the most dramatic example of a testament to Akiva's almost otherworldly intellectual brilliance, and it fits well with the notion that what we see in these stories is Akiva's self-creation.

Akiva is a complex character in these stories. His intelligence is extraordinary, and possibly his ego as well. Yet what most remains, to my mind, is his hunger to change his life, to go down a different path, to discover what will be revealed to him by his study of Torah. Perhaps the story about biting like a donkey is a later accretion, as scholars would certainly point out. But there seems to be truth in it as well. When Akiva sees water creating that well and understands that he needs to find a different way of being, we the readers cannot help but feel moved.

The stories we have explored here leave many things unexplained. Most strikingly, we remain completely ignorant of Akiva's earliest life. Except for the story about the biting donkey, the mystery of his first forty years remains unsolved. Of course rabbinic sources themselves were aware of this difficulty, and we can find within the tradition examples of attempts to solve this problem by filling in the gaps in the biography.[10]

But there is another version of Akiva's origins story that has had a profound impact on the way that he has been viewed. It is not about the Akiva who turned to Torah out of self-discovery, the Akiva at the well. It is about the Akiva who began his studies for a very different reason: he fell in love. We now turn to this version of the story.

3

A Love Story

Of all the tales about the origins of Akiva, the most famous by far is the story of Akiva's romance with his wife. One need only look at the retelling of his early life in children's books, whether they be from the 1930s, the 1950s, or the last years of the twentieth century, to see the persistence of this story.[1] Across time and despite the changes in perception, the tale of Akiva and his wife remains the version told and retold. And it is no wonder. The romantic narrative has many of the elements of a traditional fairy tale, and if Akiva's life story were presented today in a Hollywood movie, the love story version is how it would be told. Or, as we will see, at least part it.

The main story appears in two places within the Babylonian Talmud and can be supplemented with details from other sources in the rabbinic canon. The two talmudic versions are fairly close in how they tell the story, though we will explore some of the significant differences as we look at the tale.

The core stories about Akiva's romance are found in the tractates Ketubot ("Marriage Contracts" 62b–63a) and Nedarim ("Vows" 50a). The story in Ketubot begins:

> Rabbi Akiva was a shepherd of Ben Kalba Savua. Ben Kalba Savua's daughter saw how modest and outstanding Akiva was and she said to him, "If I agreed to marry you, would you go to study with a rabbi?"[2]
>
> "Yes," he replied.
>
> She was then secretly betrothed to him and sent him away to study with a rabbi. When her father heard what she had done, he threw her out of his house and vowed that she would not benefit from his wealth.
>
> b. Ketubot 62b–63a

We are in familiar territory here—the love story, the simple but noble shepherd, the wealthy landowner's daughter, and the daughter's banishment[3]—we've seen this story before, in folktales and films. It's the Western with the rich cattle lord, the beautiful daughter, and the poor cowboy working on the ranch. It's the fairy tale of the king's daughter locked in a tower and the worthy but impoverished young man trying to reach her.

In the last chapter we explored Akiva's self-creation as a sage. He stood by a well and understood his need to study Torah. Here the story is motivated by the unnamed daughter of Ben Kalba Savua. It is she who chooses Akiva; it is she who makes the proposal. She recognizes his modesty and his outstanding qualities, and she is the one who takes action.

In the text above I use the word "betrothed" to describe their relationship. Some modern translations prefer to say that the couple "got engaged"; but engagement in our modern sense is too casual a word to describe the nature of marriage customs in the ancient Jewish world, and so I prefer the old-fashioned term "betrothed." The marriage process in rabbinic law involved two stages: betrothal (called *kiddushin* or *eruvin* in Hebrew) and the wedding itself (called *nissuin* or *huppah* in Hebrew). These two events could be separated by as much as a year.[4] But the *kiddushin* phase (and this is the term that is used in the text above) was not a small matter. From the time of betrothal, the man and woman were in essence legally married; only divorce (or death) could end the marriage. The second stage seems to represent the sexual consummation of the marriage.[5]

What, we might wonder, was the purpose of having the betrothal stage at all? Couldn't a couple have just created a civil contract of intent with monetary penalties? One scholarly speculation about this question is relevant to our story: once betrothed, a woman is no longer under the legal control of her father in a world in which women (especially unmarried women) had few economic rights or legal power.[6] This idea may shed some light on our story of Akiva and the daughter of Ben Kalba Savua.

It's interesting that Akiva is described with the word "modesty." The Talmud uses an Aramaic word derived from the Hebrew *tzanua*, a term for modesty often connected to the idealized qualities of a woman. There is a kind of gender reversal here: Akiva is the modest one; he is wooed by *her*, and she sets the terms for the marriage. And it is she who takes an action that she must have known would estrange her from her father. Interestingly, the root *tzanua* also has the meaning of "in secret," as if the text wants us to make the connection between Akiva's personal quality of modesty and his secret betrothal.

Akiva's father-in-law is named Ben Kalba Savua, and he appears a few times in rabbinic literature. At times he is called Kalba Savua; at other times, *Ben* Kalba Savua, meaning *the son of* Kalba Savua. Scholars assume that these are not two different people, but simply different versions of the same name. Often, Ben Kalba Savua is mentioned alongside two other men, Ben Tzitzit Hakeset and Nakdimon ben Gorion. These three were men of great wealth and prominence, living at the time of the Great Revolt against the Roman occupation. The Midrash on Ecclesiastes (7:19), for example, says that each of these three was capable of supplying enough food for Jerusalem to survive ten years during a siege. Hence the Babylonian Talmud (b. Gittin "Decrees of Divorce" 56a) tells us that the riches of these three men allowed the city to withstand the Roman attack (until a radical element among the Jews undid their work).

In describing Kalba Savua the Talmud offers an explanation for the meaning of his name: "He was called Kalba Savua because a person could go to his house as hungry as a dog [Aramaic *kalba* from Hebrew *kelev*, meaning dog] and come out satiated [Hebrew *savua*, meaning satisfied]" (b. Gittin 56a). Both this etiology of his name and his support of the city in its time of crisis give us a picture of a man of great generosity, attuned to the hungry and the needy. In that case how do we understand his angry opposition to his daughter's marriage to Akiva?

Perhaps this is simply the very human trait of a person applying different standards when he thinks about the world at large than when events affect his own family: I'm happy to support the poor and the needy—I just don't want them to marry my daughters! This is not a particularly noble quality, but we recognize its familiarity. And it raises another question: How are we to understand Akiva's social class and economic standing? The stories discussed in the last chapter give no indication of Akiva's coming from a disadvantaged background. In fact, we know nothing about his upbringing: he is simply a man who happens upon a well. But the notion of Akiva as coming from poverty is one that is part of his image down through Jewish history, and there is good reason for that.

If we pick up the love story from its *other* telling in the Talmud, in Tractate Nedarim, we learn more about Akiva's economic situation:

The daughter of Kalba Savua betrothed herself to Rabbi Akiva. When her father heard about it, he vowed that she would not benefit from his wealth. She went and married Akiva. In the winter they slept in a hayloft, and in the mornings he picked the straw from her hair. "If only I could," he said to her, "I would give you a 'Jerusalem of Gold.'"

b. Nedarim 50a

This version of the story begins abruptly. There is no indication of why she wanted to marry him as there is in the other talmudic story, and, much more importantly, there is no *precondition* of Torah learning that she demands of him. She betroths herself to him (as in the other version, she, not Akiva, is the one described as taking action), and by doing so she engenders her father's anger. Her father cuts her off monetarily, and, without pausing for a breath, our text moves from "she would not benefit from his wealth" to "she went and married Akiva." There is something wonderfully decisive about that move. She hears her father's words; she defies him. For readers familiar with English literature, there is the unmistakable resonance of the famous line from the end of *Jane Eyre:* "Reader, I married him." And so she did.

Note that in these stories Akiva's wife has no name—she is called "the daughter of [Ben] Kalba Savua." In fact, the only place in early rabbinic literature that we are told her name is in Version A of Avot de Rabbi Natan where we read that although Akiva had no merit from social status or ancestry, "his wife Rachel had merit." (In time, later tradition adopted the usage of the name Rachel for Akiva's wife despite this single attribution, and it became conventional to refer to her as Rachel, in essence harmonizing the various versions of the story.)

Akiva and his new wife do not have an easy life. It is winter and they are sleeping in an unheated hayloft. The story in Nedarim gives us very little background to Akiva's situation, but here it makes sense to piece it together with the parallel story that we've seen in the Ketubot text and assume that Akiva is merely a worker in the employ of the wealthy Kalba Savua. Akiva is a simple shepherd, and we should not be surprised that without any family support, the couple find themselves struggling, living in a shed for storing straw. Notice also that this version of the story, unlike what we saw in the last chapter, does not describe Akiva as being forty years old. Indeed, both talmudic versions give us an image of a *young* man, at the beginning of life, certainly an unmarried man and obviously attractive to this young woman. The two Akivas—the forty-year-old with a son that we saw in Avot de Rabbi Natan and the young shepherd catching the eye of the boss's daughter—are not easily compatible. These are clearly separate traditions.

But there is some overlap nonetheless. The story in Avot de Rabbi Natan gives us some hints about Akiva's possible poverty as well, though not as obviously as what we see in the two talmudic versions:

> They said of Akiva that he did not engage in a laborer's work [once he began to study Torah] but rather he would gather two bundles of wood.[7] He would take one bundle to the market and sell it there. The other he would take home and use to make a fire to keep warm. His neighbors complained to him: "Akiva, you are killing us with the smoke! Sell your bundle of wood and buy oil with the proceeds" [to light a lamp instead of a fire]. He replied to them: "I'm not going to listen to you. I get two good things from the wood. First, I can keep warm by it, and second, I can get light from it."

> Avot de Rabbi Natan, Version B, chapter 12 (a similar story appears in Version A, chapter 6)

The story appears right after Akiva's decision to begin his studies, and obviously it is meant to communicate the idea that the time he devoted to study was so important to him that he gave up regular work. In essence, he took on a practice, if not a vow, of poverty. Of course this story tells us little about what Akiva's economic situation was before his decision to become a student of Torah, and it seems that the real cause of his poverty in the version of Avot de Rabbi Natan is due to his single-minded pursuit of learning. This is a story meant to teach about the sacrifices a great scholar is willing to make in the name of his studies.

But there is enough ambiguity here to allow us some latitude in seeing a connection between the two traditions, that of the Talmud and that of Avot de Rabbi Natan. Immediately following the story of the bundles of wood in Avot de Rabbi Natan Version B, we read a text that uses Akiva as an example of the importance of studying Torah. At the end of life when a person is called to judgment, the question will be asked, "Why did you not study Torah when you were in this world?" If the person answers, "Because I was poor," the response from the heavenly judge will be, "But Rabbi Akiva was poor." If the person says, "My ancestors laid up no merit for me," then the person will be told, "Rabbi Akiva's ancestors also did not lay up merit for him." "Because of that," the text continues, "Rabbi Akiva will shame many—all who did not study Torah in this world" (Avot de Rabbi Natan, Version B, chapter 12).[8]

Akiva is a model for dedication to Torah learning, but this text also reveals an image of Akiva's *origins* in poverty. Not only that, but the clause "Rabbi Akiva's ancestors also did not lay up merit for him" is the rabbinic way of saying that Akiva did not come from a family background distinguished by either lineage or exemplary behavior. Although this text comes from the traditions of Avot de Rabbi Natan, perhaps there is an echo of the talmudic stories about why Ben Kalba Savua may have been outraged by his daughter's decision to marry Akiva—he was a man without money, ancestry, or a good family name. As we will see, Akiva's undistinguished family background appears in traditions in the Talmud as well.

Although the version of the story told in the tractates Ketubot and Nedarim differ, two main common elements show a thematic unity between them: the rejecting father and the head-strong, perhaps even powerful, daughter. Whether one looks at the story in the light of Akiva's first- and second-century CE world or from the perspective of sixth-century Babylonia, the time of the composition of the Talmud, marriage practice by and large involved the father of the bride and not the daughter at all. Fathers arranged their daughters' marriages—and might possibly have benefited financially from the arrangement as well;[9] therefore, the presentation here of Ben Kalba Savua's daughter's activism in making this match is quite extraordinary. Indeed, no other story in rabbinic literature shows a Jewish woman arranging a marriage for herself. Rabbi Akiva's wife, in the words of the scholar Tal Ilan, "took the initiative and proposed to her husband."[10]

The story of Akiva and his wife has a number of other interesting elements. First, it is a strikingly *romantic* picture. The picture of the struggling young couple, living in poverty in a hayloft in the winter, is like a scene from an opera by Puccini. In particular we are struck by the tender and intimate gesture of Akiva picking the straw out of his wife's hair in the morning. It is almost a cinematic moment—a close-up of the young couple in love.

He tells her he would buy her a "Jerusalem of Gold" if only he could. This phrase has occasioned a good deal of scholar-ship, exploring both the textual meaning and the real-life ana-logues of the words. It turns out that "Jerusalem of Gold" is referring to a piece of expensive jewelry, something that the impoverished couple could not imagine they would ever be able to afford. But Akiva's love for his wife moves him to wish for the means to adorn her properly.

In a few places the Mishnah mentions another piece of women's jewelry called a "City of Gold." The term "Jerusalem of Gold" does not appear in the early (Mishnaic) texts; but in later texts such as the Babylonian Talmud, "Jerusalem of Gold" is used, sometimes to explain the meaning of the term "City of Gold" used in the earlier sources. In other words, in the early stages of rabbinic Judaism, City of Gold was a well-known piece of adornment; later, Jerusalem of Gold became the common term, probably for the same or very similar item.

No matter which term we use, the item is what is known as a "mural crown"—a tiara that uses the turreted outline of ancient city walls to form its shape. Such items were found on statues depicting goddesses (especially the patron goddess of a particular city) in the ancient Mediterranean world. An excellent example is in the collection of the J. Paul Getty Museum, which has a statue of the goddess Cybele wearing a mural crown, dating from around the time of Akiva's birth.

Tiaras of gold, often shaped in the form of a city wall, were given as gifts to men who first climbed the walls of a conquered city and to women who were civic patrons of institutions in a particular community. The scholar Susan Marks has suggested that we should view Akiva's wish to give his wife a Jerusalem of Gold as not only a sign of their private romance, but a symbolic indication of thanks for her being Akiva's "patron," supporting his efforts to study Torah—a communally valued activity.[11]

Rabbinic tradition sees Akiva as a person who eventually attained great wealth over time. The Jerusalem Talmud reports the following gossipy story later in his life:

> Rabbi Akiva made a "City of Gold" for his wife. Rabban Gamaliel's wife saw her and was jealous. She came and told her husband about it. Rabban Gamaliel replied, "Have you done for me what she did for him!? Rabbi Akiva's wife sold the braids of her hair and used the proceeds so that he could go study Torah."
>
> y. Sotah "The Suspected Adulteress" 9:15 (y. Shabbat "Sabbath" tells almost the exact same story)

Statue of the mother goddess Cybele (detail) wearing
a mural crown, ca. 50 CE (Courtesy of the
J. Paul Getty Museum)

Rabban Gamaliel was the leader of the Jewish community in
Palestine immediately after the destruction of Jerusalem and
therefore was an older contemporary of Akiva. We do see an
interesting additional detail added here. Gamaliel tells his wife
about the great sacrifice that Akiva's wife made for Akiva: she
sold her braids so that the family could support Akiva's study.
And even though the story about selling the braids is from a
completely different source than the story about the poor cou-

ple in the hayloft (the Jerusalem Talmud for the first, and the Babylonian Talmud for the second), the literary reader today cannot help but connect the two stories and the hair motif—that is, Akiva picking straw out of his wife's hair in one, and his wife selling her hair in the other; the *wish* for a Jerusalem of Gold in one, and her *wearing* a City of Gold in the other.[12]

Returning to our story in Tractate Nedarim, we need to explore the question of Akiva's motivation to begin his quest to learn Torah. In the last chapter we saw Akiva inspired by his experience at the well. We saw the version of the story told in the Babylonian Talmud tractate Ketubot in which Ben Kalba Savua's daughter sets the condition that he must go study in order for her to agree to marry him. In the Nedarim telling of the story, however, we get another, and surprising, element—a miraculous appearance:

> Later Elijah came to them [Akiva and his wife] appearing in the guise of an ordinary person, and cried out at the door, "Give me some straw, for my wife is giving birth, and I have nothing for her to lie down on."
>
> "See," Rabbi Akiva said to his wife, "there is a man who does not even have straw."
>
> She said to him, "Go—become a rabbi." He went and studied with Rabbi Eliezer and Rabbi Joshua for twelve years.
>
> b. Nedarim 50a

The prophet Elijah has held a powerful grasp on Jewish imagination since biblical times. His prophetic activities are detailed in 1 and 2 Kings, but as important as his deeds were, the mysterious manner of his departing the world was even more gripping. Standing with his disciple (and successor) Elisha by the banks of the Jordan, "a fiery chariot with fiery horses suddenly appeared and separated one from the other; and Elijah went up to heaven in a whirlwind" (2 Kings 2:11). Elijah does not die—he is transported into the heavens. In essence, he becomes an immortal figure, appearing in human form in many legends.

What we see in the story from Nedarim is the appearance of this mythic figure precisely at the time when Akiva is at his lowest point—locked in poverty and, we might imagine, without hope. Elijah as the bearer of hope is a typical motif in rabbinic literature—and indeed Elijah appears in a number of stories in talmudic literature, specifically to rabbis who are in trouble.[13]

In our story, unlike some of the other tales in which the prophet appears to rabbis, it is not clear what precisely Elijah does to turn Akiva toward a life of study. We have the picture of his and his wife's poverty in winter in the hayloft, the straw in her hair, the wish for the Jerusalem of Gold, the appearance of Elijah; and then without any other transition, we see Akiva's wife instructing Akiva to go study. Elijah certainly never tells Akiva that he must go learn Torah. Elijah's appearance only serves to highlight the fact that although the young couple is in dire straits, others are worse off.

Once again, it is Akiva's wife who takes action; it is she who directs Akiva to leave. In some way Elijah's visit leads her to recognize that their circumstances, as bad as they might be, are not catastrophic, that some people suffer more than they do, and this allows her to send him away. What we don't know is what happens between the lines. Has Akiva been saying that this is what he wanted to do and she has been holding him back, perhaps out of fear, given their poverty? Or does she understand that within him—perhaps unknown to himself—is a talent for Torah that is waiting to be released? We have no evidence either way, but personally, I prefer the second reading. And perhaps there is enough in the text to support it, albeit indirectly.

Remember that in the other talmudic version of the story

(b. Ketubot 62b), Ben Kalba Savua's daughter will not marry Akiva unless he studies Torah. Once again, she is the one pushing him in that direction. In both talmudic versions, I think it is fair to infer that she has seen something in him beyond his physical form—namely, that he is "modest and outstanding." She recognizes his immense potential, perhaps even more than this modest man can see it in himself. The visit of Elijah allows her to take the risk and send Akiva to fulfill his destiny. And as the other talmudic text tells us, she sells her hair to allow it to happen.

How are we to view the selling of her hair? As one scholar has pointed out, "Women's hair obviously had an erotic connotation in antiquity and was rarely let loose in public."[14] We have also seen the erotic overtones in the description of Akiva picking the straw out of his wife's hair. Clearly, Akiva's wife's decision to sell her braids was more than a simple monetary calculation; it was a deeply personal, even intimate gesture.

Both stories from the Babylonian Talmud agree in most details about what comes next. Akiva goes off to learn and stays away for twelve years. Here is how the story continues in Tractate Ketubot:

> He went and spent twelve years studying. When he returned home, twelve thousand students came with him. He heard an old man saying to [Akiva's wife], "How long will you continue to be a living widow?"
>
> She replied to the old man, "If he would listen to me, he would stay another twelve years!"
>
> Rabbi Akiva said, "So I am doing this with her consent!" He returned to his studies and stayed another twelve years. When he came back home he brought with him twenty-four thousand students.
>
> His wife heard and went out to meet him. The women in the neighborhood said to her, "Borrow some nice clothes and cover yourself."

She quoted a verse to them: "A righteous man knows the life of his beast" (Proverbs 12:10).

When she came close to Akiva, she fell on her face and kissed his feet. His students started to push her away, but Akiva said to them, "Let her go! What's mine and yours are hers!"

Her father heard that a great man had come to town and he said to himself, "I will go to this great man and perhaps he can annul the vow that I made" [that his daughter not benefit from his wealth]. So he went to him. Rabbi Akiva said to him, "If you had known that your daughter's husband was a great man, would you have made that vow?"

Ben Kalba Savua said to him, "If he had known only one chapter, or even only one law, I would not have made that vow!"

Akiva said to him: "I am he!"

Ben Kalba Savua fell on his face, kissed Akiva's feet, and gave him half of his wealth.

b. Ketubot 62b–63a

This section of the story is complex from a literary perspective in many ways. For one thing, the narrator is balancing a number of different characters—Akiva, his wife, the unnamed "old man," the unnamed "women in the neighborhood," Akiva's students, and Ben Kalba Savua—along with two time frames: Akiva's return after twelve years and his *second* return after an additional twelve years. On top of that the narrator is juggling the reader's point of view: from seeing the world, back and forth, through the eyes of the wife, Akiva, and Ben Kalba Savua in a kind of cinematic "cross-cutting."

This part of the story revolves around the question of what it means to know, to really understand, another person. The theme gets expressed through the medium of speech—indirect and direct, overheard and face-to-face. The "old man" speaks to Akiva's wife, perhaps even taunts her, as being abandoned by her husband for all these years. Like the women in the neighborhood, he represents the vox populi, the "word on the street" about Akiva and his wife. The parallel version told in Tractate Nedarim makes an even more pointed judgment about this anonymous voice in his wife's ear, calling him "a wicked man" who tells her that Ben Kalba Savua was right to object to her marriage and treat her as he did. Akiva, the wicked man tells her, is "not like you"; that is, Akiva was her inferior in social status, and he abandoned her to a veritable widowhood for years.

But she is unmoved by what the man says. From her point of view, Akiva should spend *another* twelve years in study! Akiva overhears her and realizes that he has her consent to continue learning. The fact that the text reports him saying to himself, "So I am doing this with her consent!" leaves the impression that perhaps Akiva was wondering about what she was thinking about his extended stay away from her. But indeed, he has had her consent all along.

He returns to his teachers and stays another twelve years. Note that the wife's conversation with the old man happens directly, but it is *indirectly* heard by Akiva. At this point we the readers are perplexed about how to read this interaction. Doesn't the old man (wicked or not) voice our own view of the situation? *Hasn't* Akiva abandoned her to a kind of widowhood? Yet, as the story proceeds, we see that in the case of Akiva and his wife, mere indirect speech is enough to communicate understanding. The *direct* speech of the old man and of the neighbors is what denotes a lack of knowledge. They don't understand that she really does want Akiva to be away studying; they don't understand that wearing fine clothes for her reunion with her husband doesn't matter, to her or to him. The deep connection between them was forged when they were rebels against her father, living in the hayloft in winter.

In the same way, Akiva's students don't understand the situation either. They see this woman and start to push her away.

But of course, Akiva immediately knows who she is, and more than that he says to them, "What's mine and yours are hers!" In other words, everything that he has learned and therefore everything that *they* have learned from him really belongs to her, because she made it possible for Akiva to become the "great man" (as the text emphasizes) that he has become.

This story presents some obvious difficulties for readers today. First, we are uncomfortable, deeply uncomfortable I would say, with the image of the self-sacrificing wife giving up her happiness (having to be a "living widow") and material comforts (having to borrow nice clothes) just to support her man in his vocation. Second, Akiva abandoning her for twenty-four years seems monstrous to us. Thus, we understand the view of the "old man"—we share that view today. Third, the verse from Proverbs that she uses to justify her behavior to the neighbors is unsettling—is she really comparing herself to a beast owned by this "righteous man"?

These are certainly troubling issues, and we should not ignore them, but we can be helped by viewing these materials through the lens of rabbinic culture in ancient times. That world, it goes without saying, was very different from the one in which we live today, and those differences are particularly striking when we look at the role and status of women in a male-dominated culture. Akiva is an unusual figure in rabbinic lore precisely because his wife is accorded such a significant role in his development. Tal Ilan, a feminist scholar of these materials, has devoted a good deal of analysis to the stories of Akiva's wife, and she concludes that the "persistent element" of her role reflects the fact that Akiva's "fame, unlike that of his colleagues, was in fact achieved with the help of his wife. Exactly what she did, how she helped, what support she rendered him, we do not know. But whatever it was, it must have been substantial if it left such an imprint on the minds of storytellers."[15] The story, at least as far as we know, was written and shaped by men. Men originally told these tales orally, and eventually they were written down and edited by the unnamed men whom scholars today call the *Stamma'im*, a modern term that essentially means "anonymous ones."[16] So for those reasons alone we should not be surprised that Akiva's wife is valorized for sacrificing herself to a man's needs.

But we should also remember that "his needs" is an inadequate and much more personalized way of stating what Akiva accomplished in the eyes of the Talmud's later redactors. To their minds he is a heroic figure, a person who both preserved and advanced the entire enterprise of Jewish life and culture. He saved the future of the Jewish people and shaped Jewish religion for all time. To them, the criticism that Akiva should not have left his wife would be tantamount to the belief that George Washington should never have left his farm in Virginia to lead the Continental Army because in doing so he abandoned his family and left them to face hard times alone during the Revolutionary War. Akiva saying, "What's mine and yours are hers!" is enormous praise. The reader is meant to understand that he is not paying lip service. He means it.

Akiva abandons his wife for twenty-four years; there is no way around that. As important as that might have been for Jewish history, she is left alone, and the attitude of the "old man" and the neighbors makes it clear to us that she must have suffered, even though she believed in what he was doing. How are we to understand the issue of Akiva abandoning his wife?

It is important to examine the context in the Talmud in which this story is related. It appears among a set of stories over the course of a few pages in the Babylonian Talmud in which the rabbis are debating the question of the sexual obligations of husbands to their wives. What frequency of sexual intercourse must a man provide for his wife? Some might be surprised to see such a question in the pages of the Talmud, but it is a work that is involved with a remarkably wide range of human behaviors, and this particular question is one that is framed in the earliest stages of rabbinic culture. The Mishnah (Ketubot 5:6) states that Torah students—with the permission of their wives—can leave their homes to study for a maximum of thirty days. (Other men, depending on their occupations, are allowed either longer or shorter periods of abstinence.)

The Talmud scholar Daniel Boyarin has analyzed the pages in Tractate Ketubot in the Babylonian Talmud in which this statement from the Mishnah is explored. In the course of the Talmud's discussion, no fewer than six stories on a single page about various sages are brought to elucidate the proper behavior of rabbis to their wives in regard to sexual obligations. All the stories deal with the conflict, as Boyarin succinctly puts it, between "sex and the text."[17] As he points out, the issue of scholars leaving home to spend time in the Beit Midrash, leaving their wives behind, was a matter of complex internal conflict within the values of rabbinic culture. Of course by the time of the Babylonian Talmud, Torah study was held in higher regard than virtually anything else in Jewish life; yet at the same time, marriage was constantly praised and valued in rabbinic literature.

Part of what we are seeing in these pages of the Talmud, Boyarin demonstrates, is a contrast between two different models of dealing with the problem of sex and the text. In the Jewish community in Eretz Yisrael, the practice was for rabbis to delay marriage and spend their time in study *before* marrying. But the Babylonian tradition found this approach wanting. In that view, sexual desire would be too distracting for young scholars, so early marriages were encouraged. But this solution had its own profound difficulties because in essence it created a class of individuals that Boyarin memorably calls "married monks."[18] How would these rabbis negotiate their obligations at home and their investment in learning?

The multiple stories on pages 63a–63b of Tractate Ketubot

all represent various attempts to deal with this conflict of time and commitments. Most of the stories present examples of abysmal, and at times tragic, failure. One rabbi, Rav Rehumi, fails to come home to visit his wife (he would come home only once a year, and in this particular year he was so engrossed in study that he forgot to come home at all). The ironic consequence is that the roof upon which he is sitting while studying collapses, and he dies. (To make sense of the scene we need to picture a flat roof, as is typical of Mediterranean settings.) In another case R. Hananiah ben Hakinai spends so much time away from home that when he returns for a visit, he cannot find his own house. R. Hama ben Bisa returns home and does not recognize his own son, who has grown up during his absence.

It is at this point, after these other tales have been told, that our story about Akiva appears. Interestingly, and obviously with great intention of the editors, both Hanania ben Hakinai and Hama ben Bisa have spent twelve years away in study—the same amount of time that appears in the Akiva tale. But unlike their situations and unlike the tragic case of Rav Rehumi, Akiva's return and his relationship with his wife are seen as so successful that she sends him away for another twelve years. The editors of the Talmud have cleverly called upon the prestige of Akiva, one of the great figures of the Jewish community in Eretz Yisrael, to justify the practice of the "married monks" of Babylonia. Because the weight of earlier Jewish tradition had asserted that even scholars, whose vocation is so admired, cannot spend more than a month away from their wives, the authorities in the Babylonian Talmud needed to find an extremely powerful figure to justify the practice of married monks. For as Boyarin puts it, "symbols with great cultural authority were necessary, and there is none greater in Jewish tradition than Rabbi Akiva."[19]

Akiva, as we will see many times, is often the decisive person in a debate or represents the clinching argument made through personal example. In the story of Akiva and his wife, they are exemplifying the Babylonian idealized model: the husband who becomes a great man, and the wife who not only accepts but encourages his absence.

The picture of deep connection between Akiva and his wife evidenced in these stories is disturbed, perhaps even undermined, for the modern reader by her use of the verse from Proverbs to explain their relationship. She has no need to put on fancy clothes, she tells her neighbors, because "a righteous man knows the life of his beast" (Proverbs 12:10). Is she saying that she is like a mere animal? Is she saying that Akiva "owns" her the way a person might own an animal?

To be sure, we are looking at an ancient culture that, like many others of its time, viewed women in a subservient role to men. There is no avoiding that fact. But there are certain complicating if not mitigating factors at play here as well. Boyarin sees the tale as an extended metaphor in which Akiva is the shepherd and his wife is his "beloved ewe." He links the name of Akiva's wife that is given in Avot de Rabbi Natan—Rachel, in Hebrew *Rahel*, a word meaning sheep or ewe—to the story we have here in the Babylonian Talmud. As we have seen, in the talmudic stories that we have been considering, Akiva's wife remains unnamed; it is only in Avot de Rabbi Natan that we learn the name Rachel. But, Boyarin argues, we are meant to hear an association with that name because on the next page of the Talmud immediately following the Akiva story, we are told an anecdote about Akiva's daughter behaving in a way similar to her mother. To explain the connection between mother and daughter, the Talmud quotes a proverb that puns off of the name (and word) *Rahel:* "Ewe follows ewe; a daughter's acts are like those of her mother." Boyarin argues that the talmudic story is based on shepherd and ewe imagery, making it somewhat less unpleasant for modern readers. For Boyarin puts it, "The metaphor of male lover as shepherd and female beloved as ewe is, in fact, common in biblical discourse, used frequently as a figure for the relationship of God and Israel and appearing often in the Song of Songs."[20]

None of this changes the fundamental power imbalance in the relationship of the man and woman, of course. The wife is subservient to the husband as the ewe is subservient to the shepherd. But seeing the connection to the biblical imagery of the relationship between God and Israel ("the Lord is my shepherd," for example) may help mitigate some of the negativity that Akiva's wife's reference to Proverbs may elicit in us today.

Another interesting perspective on the use of the quotation from Proverbs—and perhaps one that is more convincing—is offered by the Talmud scholar Shamma Friedman.[21] His work is a beautiful example of the ways in which meticulous academic scholarship can enlighten the meaning of an ancient text. Friedman, examining manuscript versions of texts that quote our Akiva story in other works, shows that the quotation that the wife uses in the talmudic text may in fact not be the verse that was originally intended. Rather than Proverbs 12:10, these other manuscripts quote Proverbs 29:7, which has a similar structure but a completely different meaning: "A righteous man is concerned with the cause of the wretched." If this is indeed the verse that should appear here, it makes a good deal of sense. Rather than Akiva's wife saying, "Akiva will recognize me despite my humble clothing because the master always knows his own animal," she is saying, "I don't need to be wearing fancy clothing; being a righteous and compassionate man, Akiva will care about my wretched and downtrodden state." This casts a very different light on their reunion. And in the context of Akiva's rebuke of his students—everything we are, is thanks to her—this quotation from Proverbs is particularly apt.

The story ends by bringing events full circle through the reconciliation of Akiva and his father-in-law. The fairy-tale feel of the story is only intensified by this ending. But the last scene also continues the theme of knowledge and true understanding that we have been examining. Kalba Savua did not recognize Akiva's abilities when Akiva was young, and now he quite *literally* fails to recognize Akiva when the great scholar stands before him. It seems clear that the Talmud wants us to see Kalba Savua in a negative light by presenting these events in such a symbolically resonant fashion. Moreover, a darker side to his character may be embodied in his very name. Earlier I quoted the explanation of "Kalba Savua" given in both the Babylonian Talmud and Avot de Rabbi Natan: "a person could go to his house as hungry as a dog and come out satiated." But there is another and in fact more literal translation of his name—that is, "satisfied dog." Is that who the man is supposed to be?—not the paragon of generosity who tried to save Jerusalem during the siege before its destruction, but rather a smug, self-satisfied snob who refuses to let his daughter marry the love of her life and goes so far as to banish her from his house.

Judging Kalba Savua, however, is not so easy. We can sympathize with his wanting to do well by his daughter, but we wonder whether perhaps his concern is more for his own social status than for his daughter's welfare. He was, after all, quick to cut off her finances and send her away from his home. We don't know much about her own motivations. Perhaps she was a rebellious teenager, out to goad her father by pushing the limits of respectability. Perhaps she felt constrained by a domineering father and wanted to break away. Her choice of Akiva was sure to infuriate her father, and that is precisely what she might have intended.

Still, it is hard to view her as a rebellious rich girl looking to stir the overly bourgeois and conventional pot at home, given the very positive light in which she is presented in the stories we have examined. We don't see any of that negativity in the portrait of her married life. One wonders whether the hard-knocks life in a cold hayloft may have tamed whatever irresponsible impulses were within her. When she saw Elijah in the guise of a poor man, she came face to face with the real difficulties of poverty. She was no longer living in luxury, true; but others were far worse off than she was. She becomes a person willing to sacrifice for a larger cause.

And what of her father? No matter how we view his relationship with his daughter in her youth, his treatment in rejecting her is despicable. But as this story ends, we are given some redemptive hints about Kalba Savua. Most telling is the fact that he is hoping to annul the vow of rejection that he made all those years ago (by the calculus of this story, it has to be at least twenty-four years, of course). In talmudic culture a vow is not a casual matter. Indeed, many pages of the Talmud are devoted to the complexity of the issue of vows—what constitutes a vow and in what way a vow can be nullified. Kalba Savua hears that a great sage has come to town and goes to discover from this sage how he might rid himself of the vow he made years ago, "that she would not benefit from his wealth." Of course he has no idea that the great sage is Akiva himself. The fact that the story emphasizes his regret, his desire to undo the past, casts a different light on Kalba Savua. He may be a "satisfied dog," but in this case it appears that he is bothered by the foolish words that came out of his mouth when his daughter announced that she wanted to marry Akiva. He thus becomes a considerably more complex character in the reader's eyes.

And the fact that he values Torah learning also adds to his credit. Akiva asks him, "If you had known that your daughter's husband was a great man, would you have made that vow?" By "great man" we are to understand "great in learning"—not great in wealth or social status, but great in Torah. That is clear from Kalba Savua's answer: "If he had known only one chapter, or even only one law, I would not have made that vow!" Immediately upon hearing those words, Akiva reveals himself. It seems that the acknowledgment of the importance of learning is precisely what persuades Akiva to tell Kalba Savua the truth.

So even Kalba Savua, who seems at first to be the villain of the piece, is transformed. He too moves from uncertainty to understanding. He too comes to know Akiva for who he is. This understanding is confirmed by the gesture that Kalba Savua makes—falling on his face and kissing Akiva's feet, a sign of ultimate respect in the ancient world. More importantly, this act mimics what Akiva's wife did upon greeting Akiva. She—the one who has always *truly* known Akiva—makes the gesture that her father imitates, indicating that he too has moved toward understanding the greatness of the man who married his daughter.

On top of that, something else has dramatically changed: through his father-in-law, Akiva has now become a wealthy man (Kalba Savua gives him "half his wealth"). And with that the story of Akiva's wife comes to an end. She essentially drops out of rabbinic literature—we have the stories of her meeting and marrying Akiva, of her welcoming him back after twelve and then twenty-four years, and of Rabban Gamaliel's wife being jealous of her jewelry. There are some stories about the couple's children, but virtually none about her aside from these. This is curious, particularly after the importance of her role in the formation of Akiva as a scholar. But perhaps we are meant to understand that the spotlight now shifts to him. His world is the world of his colleagues in the early period of rabbinic Judaism. In the next chapter we explore those relationships. But before we move on, there is one strange coda to our story: the tale of Akiva's *other* wife.

There are two places in the Babylonian Talmud in which Akiva is said to have married a second time. Clearly, this must have taken place after the death of his wife (polygamy was not expressly forbidden by Jewish law in rabbinic times, but monogamy seems to have been the norm), although as I've said, there is no reference to her dying in any other stories. Nonetheless, the surprising thing about Akiva's second marriage is the woman whom he married. The story about this possible

second marriage is told obliquely, as if by hints. The first instance comes in a discussion of an issue mentioned above—the
fact that Akiva was said to have become wealthy later in his
life, and rabbinic literature is interested in the sources of that
wealth. The most obvious one is through Kalba Savua, as we
have seen. But along with that answer, five other options are
also given in the discussion, some quite fanciful, such as Akiva
finding a trunk filled with coins that had washed up on shore
from a shipwreck, or returning a missing hoard of treasure to
a Roman matron who rewarded him for his honesty. But the
most surprising of all of these is that he became wealthy by
marrying the former wife of Turnus Rufus, the Roman governor of Judaea! This bombshell appears without any further clarification in Tractate Nedarim (50a–b). In a different tractate,
however, we learn a bit more about this bizarre tale.

The story appears in the midst of a discussion about whether
a Jew is allowed to praise the beauty of a pagan woman. One
rabbi says that it is not allowed—how can we praise a person who
worships idols? Rabbi Shimon ben Gamaliel, however, is reported to have seen a "pagan woman who was particularly beautiful and exclaimed: 'How manifold are your works, O Lord,'"
quoting from Psalm 104:24.

The Talmud continues with another example of the connection between a pagan woman and a noted rabbi:

> Likewise, when Rabbi Akiva saw the wife of the wicked Tur-
> nus Rufus, he spat, then laughed, and then wept. He spat
> because of her originating from a putrid drop. He laughed
> because he understood that in the future she would convert
> to Judaism and would become his wife. He wept because he
> understood that such beauty would eventually decay to dust.
>
> b. Avodah Zarah "Idol Worship" 20a

The interpretation of Akiva's three actions—spitting, laughing,
and weeping—is given by the anonymous narrator of the Tal-

mud. The reader is struck by two aspects of this story: first that it is told in the context of a discussion about beautiful pagan women, and second that Akiva laughs when thinking of his future marriage to this *particular* pagan woman, the wife of his adversary.

In addition, Turnus Rufus is not only an enemy of the Jewish people; he has a particular antagonism toward Akiva. Turnus Rufus is the Hebrew name in rabbinic sources (sometimes spelled as one word, "Turnusrufus") for the real-life figure Tinneius Rufus who ruled briefly at the beginning of the Bar Kokhba War (132 CE) (see chapter 7). It appears he was not particularly successful in putting down the Jewish revolt and was replaced soon afterwards. There is not a great deal of reliable historical information about Tinneius Rufus, but in rabbinic literature Turnus Rufus is seen as an evil character responsible for Roman decrees that the Jews found particularly odious. In a number of places in the Talmud he is shown engaging in debates with Akiva about matters of Jewish law and theology in which Akiva consistently defeats him. (In chapter 7 we will see his role as the villain in one version of the story of Akiva's death.)

Aside from these two references, the Talmud gives no further details about this surprising episode of Akiva's marriage to Turnus Rufus's wife, but hundreds of years later the fourteenth-century commentator Rabbenu Nissim of Gerona[22] in his commentary on Tractate Nedarim filled in the details of the story from his own imagination:

> Rabbi Akiva would debate Turnus Rufus in front of the Caesar and would always triumph. One time Turnus Rufus came home in an angry foul mood. His wife asked him, "Why is your face so angry?"
>
> He replied to her "Because of Rabbi Akiva who is defeating me every day in these debates."
>
> She said to him, "Their God hates sexual licentious-

ness. Give me your permission and I will cause him to fall into sin."

He gave his permission and she adorned herself and went to Rabbi Akiva. When he saw her, Akiva spat, laughed, and cried.

"What do these three things mean?" she asked.

Akiva replied: "I will explain two of them, but the third I will not. I spat because I know that you originated from a putrid drop. I cried because I understood that your beauty will eventually decay to dust."

He laughed because he saw through prophetic vision that in the future she would convert to Judaism and would become his wife, but he did not want to let her know that.

She asked him, "Is there any way for me to repent?"

"Yes," he answered her. So she went and converted to Judaism.

He married her and she brought great wealth into the marriage.[23]

Obviously, Rabbenu Nissim has taken the actions of Akiva from Tractate Avodah Zarah and built upon them for his commentary on Tractate Nedarim. Instead of being the words of the anonymous narrator, at least some of the words are transferred into Akiva's own voice. Of course, quite a bit is left unclear: he tells her to convert, and in the next sentence we read that Akiva is marrying her. And what happens to Turnus Rufus? Rabbenu Nissim is not interested in filling in the story; he simply wants to clarify the background to this surprising incident in Akiva's life.

We well might wonder where this story of a failed seduction came from. Once again, it is a familiar folk tradition that one can find in many cultures. It is even possible that there was such an oral tradition about the story of Akiva and Turnus Rufus and Nissim was simply writing it down. Or this may be the fruit of his own imagination, bolstered by the talmudic report of Akiva spitting, laughing, and crying. No matter what its origins, the incident of Akiva, Turnus Rufus, and Rufus's wife is fascinating—and clearly, Rabbenu Nissim found it so as well.

Of course it is hard to imagine that debates between Akiva and Turnus Rufus actually took place, but the fact that the editors of the Babylonian Talmud chose to imagine this confrontation is significant in its own way, unrelated to historical facts. The battle between the Roman governor and the Jewish sage symbolizes the battle of cultures—pagan and Jewish. Not only does Akiva consistently outwit his enemy; he ends up marrying his rival's wife, as symbolic a gesture of triumph as one can find.

Through the story of Akiva's wife we have seen how he went off to study Torah. But what happened to Akiva during those twenty-four years of study? How did he become a "great man" of Torah? And how did his colleagues relate to him? We now turn to Akiva's life among his fellow rabbis.

4

The Growth of a Scholar

TWELVE THOUSAND STUDENTS! Twenty-four thousand students! What are we to make of the number of disciples that Akiva is said to have acquired in the days before he returned home to his wife? Of course twenty-four years is a long time; still, it is not credible that even the most energetic teacher is likely to accumulate so many students (at least before the invention of the Internet!). In the matter of numbers, we are compelled to grant ancient texts—and not only Jewish sources—an exemption for what we might call hyperbolic license. So in the case of Akiva, the number of students should not be taken literally but as a way to express in figurative language his enormous influence.

The number twelve, and its multiples, is not an accidental choice, for it is a number of great symbolic resonance throughout the Bible. The number 120 (Moses's lifespan according to the Bible), or 12,000 or 24,000, is meant not only to say "a large number" (of years, of students), but to connote something else, namely, fullness and completion. The twelve months of the Jewish calendar, the twelve sons of Jacob, and the twelve tribes of Israel are all signs of the sense of wholeness associated with this number.

What remains unclear, of course, is how Akiva moved from the ignorance first attributed to him to such later prominence. No matter which story of origin we explore—the forty-year-old studying with his son or the young married man going off to learn at the urging of his wife—Akiva begins with little and attains greatness. Is there any way to see his growth as a scholar? Unfortunately, rabbinic sources do not give us an easy time on matters of chronology. We have no compact birth-to-death narratives of rabbinic figures, and sources often are at odds with one another. We have a similar difficulty in many cases with matters of geography; trying to place Akiva's life on a map is not a simple task. It is virtually impossible, in other words, to say that when Akiva was such-and-such age, he lived in such-and-such town: the paucity of information about both chronology and geography works against us. But we do have hints and fragments that offer some insight into Akiva's journey as a scholar—at least the way that tradition framed that journey in the accounts told in the Talmud and other sources.

We have seen both in the Talmud and in Avot de Rabbi Natan that Akiva went to study with Rabbi Joshua ben Hananiah and Rabbi Eliezer ben Hyrcanus. These two names appear consistently as Akiva's teachers. Tradition identifies Eliezer and Joshua as two of the five key disciples of Rabban Yohanan ben Zakkai, the leading figure in the beginnings of what came to be rabbinic Judaism. It was Yohanan, according to rabbinic texts, who preached against resistance to Rome during the First Revolt of 66–70 CE. Trapped within the walled city of Jerusalem, Yohanan escaped, as told in one of the greatest stories in all of rabbinic literature, by posing as a dead body carried out of the city in a coffin. A number of different versions of the story are told in the rabbinic canon, but the main point in each is that the coffin was brought to Vespasian, the Roman general besieging the city, and Yohanan foretold that Vespasian would become emperor of Rome. Vespasian granted Yohanan a wish in gratitude for this prediction, and, in the Talmud's version in Tractate Gittin ("Decrees of Divorce" 56a–b), Yohanan asks, "Give me Yavneh and its sages, the lineage of Rabban Gamaliel and a doctor to heal Rabbi Zadok."

Essentially, Yohanan asks to go to a place (Yavneh, or Jamnia, a city near the coast not far from Jaffe and modern Tel Aviv) to create both a center for Jewish learning and a place where the Gamaliel family and its hereditary line can continue to lead the Jewish people. Academic scholars starting back in the late 1950s have cast considerable doubt on the historicity of this tale for a variety of reasons and have come to view it less as history and more as an ideological statement about the formation period of rabbinic Judaism.[1] As one historian has put it, "the story serves as a kind of foundation myth for the post-Temple Patriarchal and Rabbinic establishment."[2]

The "Patriarch" (*Nasi* in Hebrew) was the term given to the more or less official leader of the Jews in Palestine, and the role was considered a matter of dynastic succession. Hillel was perhaps the earliest figure associated with the title (at the end of the first century BCE). His successors included Rabban Gamaliel the Elder (also known as Rabban Gamaliel I), Hillel's grandson, who even gets a mention in the New Testament; and Gamaliel the Elder's grandson, Rabban Gamaliel II, who plays a role, as we will see, in some of the important stories about Akiva.

The actual historical role of the Patriarch in these early times is extremely hazy. Many years later (probably beginning around the third century CE), the position was invested with considerable authority, thanks to recognition by the Roman rulers, and historians tend to view the traditions about the earlier figures as modes of validating the realities of the later sources' world by establishing a link to the distant past.[3] But the notion of dual strands of leadership—Torah learning and dynastic status—that is found in the legend of Yohanan's request to Vespasian is one of the story's important messages. In addition, the sheer power of the symbolism of Yohanan arising out of a coffin attests to the rabbis' view that Judaism arose out of the horrible destruction of the Temple and Jerusalem, thanks to the efforts that were undertaken by the scholars at Yavneh. The message was this: the Jewish people would survive because of the enterprise of study and the linkage to the leaders of the past.

There is also another connection of the coffin story to Akiva. How does the coffin get smuggled out of the besieged Jerusalem? Two men carry it out: Rabbi Eliezer ben Hyrcanus and Rabbi Joshua ben Hananiah. Akiva's teachers, in other words, are *his* direct link to Yohanan. Akiva's connection through his own teachers to Rabban Yohanan is important in establishing his credentials as a sage.

In Chapter 2 we saw the moment in which Akiva told his students how in his youth he was so antagonistic to the scholars that he wished he could bite them like a donkey. There is another text in which Akiva similarly looks back on his early days as a student. It appears both in the Jerusalem Talmud and in one of the so-called minor tractates of the Babylonian Talmud. This is the version in the Babylonian Talmud:

> Rabbi Akiva said: "This was the beginning of my service to the sages:
>
> "I got up early one morning and came upon a person who had been killed. I carried this body for about six thousand cubits [a little less than two miles] until I brought it to a cemetery and buried him there. When I came before the sages [the version in the Jerusalem Talmud specifically states that he came before Rabbi Eliezer and Rabbi Joshua] and

with great excitement told them what had happened, they said to me, 'Every step you took is counted as a sin against you, as if you had shed blood.' I applied the principle of *kal vahomer* and said to myself, 'If at a time when I intended to do something that would count toward my merit, I have sinned, in a case where I intended to do less, how much the more would I have sinned!'"

Whenever people reminded Rabbi Akiva of this incident, he would say, "That was how I began to gain merit!"

b. Semahot[4] "Mourning" 4:19

The version in the Jerusalem Talmud (Nazir "The Nazirite" 7:1) adds the coda: "From that moment on I always continued to serve the sages."

Let us unpack what goes on here and what lesson Akiva takes away from this peculiar incident. The context of the story in Tractate Semahot is a discussion about the obligations of *kohanim*, the hereditary category of "priests," in connection with dead bodies. The priests' main function had to do with the practice of Temple sacrifice, and because of the specialized nature of their connection to the sacred, they were forbidden by strictures already found in the Bible (for example, Leviticus 21) to come in contact with dead bodies (except for those of their closest relatives) in order not to damage the ritual purity of their vocation. Even today, religious Jews who are descendants of the priestly class avoid attending funerals for those who are not close relatives, and *kohanim* are buried in a separate section of Jewish cemeteries.

Interestingly, an exception is made for a priest coming upon an abandoned body. Tractate Semahot states, "If a priest finds an abandoned corpse, he must attend to its needs." The Talmud then goes on to discuss the category of an "abandoned corpse"—what constitutes "abandonment" and what are the obligations of both priests and others in regard to such a body?

The main thrust of the argument is that generally speaking a corpse that fits the category "abandoned" must be buried *immediately* where it is found.[5] It is at this moment in the tractate that we read the story of Akiva's remembering his past behavior.

Akiva is beginning his life as a scholar, and he happens upon a corpse. Tractate Semahot describes the body as "killed." Was it killed during war? By accident or murder? We don't know, and no further backstory is given. The version in the Jerusalem Talmud uses instead the technical term for "abandoned body" (*met mitzvah*), and it is clear by context that Tractate Semahot also intends us to understand that this slain person fits that category of "abandoned body."

Clearly Akiva knows nothing about the abandoned body category and the requirement about its immediate burial. He sees a body and does what appears on the surface to be a moral, perhaps even heroic, act: he carries the remains to a cemetery for a proper burial. And it is equally clear that he believes that he has done something exceptionally good. He is excited to tell his teachers about the act of kindness he performed for this anonymous person. But when he tells them, instead of receiving praise and encouragement, he hears a strong rebuke: "Every step you took is counted as a sin against you, as if you had shed blood." Surely, this is meant hyperbolically. Not burying an abandoned corpse in its place is certainly not equal to murder.

But in a pedagogic sense the teachers have found a way to make their point. Akiva reflects on what has happened and, in a moment that recalls his application of the talmudic principle of "how much the more so" (*kal vahomer*) during the story we discussed in chapter 2, Akiva comes to the conclusion that he was fortunate that he made his mistake while he was trying to do something good; if he had been doing something less noble and made such a mistake, he certainly would have sinned! From this time forward he vows to "serve the sages" so that he can avoid future misdeeds.

But what in fact has he learned? And why would serving the sages help him avoid such errors in the future? First, he has encountered a challenge that forces him to consider: What is the nature of the right way to live? Does he just ignore this body and not trouble himself about it, or does he try to do what is moral, inconvenient though it may be? Akiva's first instinct when he comes upon the abandoned body was to rely on two principles—his innate sense of moral behavior and his understanding of the rules of the then-evolving Jewish tradition. At the most basic human level Akiva understood that taking care of this body (and it's interesting that the Hebrew word used in the text for carrying the body [*nitpalti*] to the cemetery literally means *I took care of* the remains) meant that he could not leave it lying unburied "on the road," as the Jerusalem Talmud version describes the location. He understood in his deepest humanity that he needed to bury the body. And he understood as well that Jewish tradition deeply valued honoring the dead. To leave the body unburied would be an affront both to his inner moral being and to his understanding of Jewish principles.

But he learns from the consequences of the story that having an innate moral sensibility and a concept of Jewish ideals is not sufficient to fulfill his role as rabbi and sage. Taking the body to a cemetery seemed like precisely the right response, but he had not counted upon the subtleties and complications of Jewish law. In *this* case another principle held precedence: burying the body where it lay. This is his first education in a hard concept: Jewish practice may not always conform to one's understanding of "the right thing." Jewish tradition is about a discipline—the hard-won, hammered-out, hotly debated practices that are the essence of *halakhah*, law, or in its literal meaning, the Jewish "path." For a person as intellectually able as Akiva, this is both a challenge and an immense opportunity. He cannot rely on guesswork and instinct; he needs to join the conversation, the give-and-take of what comes to be known as "talmudic" inquiry. It is an *opportunity* because the channeling of his innate intelligence into the world of that community of debate will be the perfect realization of his talents. In that arena, in time, he will become a master.

But there is another outcome from this experience, something that also changes his life—"This was the beginning of my service to the sages." The concept of "serving the sages" (*shimmush talmidei hakhamim*, sometimes translated as "ministering to the sages" or "attending to the sages") is a powerful principle in rabbinic culture. The basic idea is that learning Torah requires becoming embedded in the *life* of Torah. To study books and ideas in the "classroom" is not sufficient. One must model one's behavior after the lives of the masters. You learn from being near sages, by watching their ways and modeling your life after those behaviors.

The Talmud points out the importance of "serving the sages" in a number of passages, emphasizing the idea that there are things that one cannot learn in books but only from living exemplars. Rabbi Akiva tells an extreme example of this in another talmudic passage: "I once followed Rabbi Joshua," Akiva relates, "into the outhouse," and he learned from how Joshua conducted himself there (b. Berakhot "Blessings" 62a). Akiva's student Ben Azzai is shocked and asks, "How did you dare to do such a thing with your master?" Akiva calmly responds, "It was a matter of Torah, and I needed to learn."

This is a far cry from learning about burying an abandoned corpse, but the text does not tell us that Rabbi Joshua protested Akiva's behavior. It appears that he understood Akiva's motivation and supported it. Indeed, the passage shows that this practice of learning from the deeds of one's teachers—even in such matters as behavior in an outhouse—is a lesson communicated well by Akiva. We are told immediately afterward that Ben Azzai told *his* student that he once followed Akiva into an outhouse! When asked the same question—"how did you dare?"—Ben

Azzai repeats his rabbi's same words, "It was a matter of Torah, and I needed to learn."

Are there no limits to learning from the rabbi's deeds? Perhaps there are. Our talmudic text relates a story immediately afterward about Rav Kahana sneaking into his master's bedroom and hiding under the bed while the rabbi and his wife were making love. When his teacher discovered him there, the master told him to leave, saying, "This is not how people are supposed to behave!" Kahana tried out the same mantra: "It was a matter of Torah, and I needed to learn." We do not hear the master's reply, but one imagines he was not pleased. Indeed, it is possible that this story is meant to be a humorous parody of the tales of Akiva and Ben Azzai following their teachers into the outhouse.[6]

No matter how we view these particular tales, there is no doubt that "serving the sages" is a lesson Akiva learned in the case of the abandoned body. Couldn't he have learned how to act upon finding an abandoned body simply by studying the relevant texts or participating in the discussions with the circle of sages? Yes, of course he could have. But Akiva's response to being rebuked was not to say, "I should have learned that lesson in class." Rather, he goes in a different direction: "I need to watch Torah as it is *embodied* by these teachers." This is not our modern idea of academic study where we aim to learn a subject from those who teach us, rather than find in them a role model for our lives.

But in Akiva's world that would not have been possible. This was not a mere academic endeavor that he was engaged in; it was mastering a way of thinking *and* a way of living his life. When he says, "From that moment on I always continued to serve the sages," he is choosing a way of being that will influence his future, both as a student and as a teacher himself as he gains followers over the years. So the story of Akiva and the abandoned body marks the beginning of two dimensions of his life: an immersion into the depths of Jewish law and practice, and a commitment to a life of lived Torah.

Akiva looks back on his early years "serving the sages," but his relationship with Rabbi Joshua ben Hananiah and Rabbi Eliezer ben Hyrcanus, his own teachers—the ones whom presumably he was "serving"—was anything but simple. As we saw in chapter 2, in the version of his early life told in Avot de Rabbi Natan, Akiva—like the stonecutter chipping away at a mountain—is portrayed as uprooting and overturning their teachings.

Of the two teachers, Akiva appears to have had a much more difficult time with Rabbi Eliezer. In chapter 2 I suggested that the placement of the Akiva and Eliezer origin stories side by side in Avot de Rabbi Natan sets up an almost structural tension between the two. At the same time, Joshua and Akiva seem more closely allied.

Disagreements among the rabbis did not always go so smoothly. Rabbinic culture presents a world dominated by the relationships among masters and disciples, teachers and students. But contrary to what we might expect, much as there is respect and reverence for the masters in that world, there is also a dominant theme of dispute and even confrontation—between teacher and student, among students themselves. The master has status and power, but even the lowliest student can challenge the master and best him by the power of the disciple's argument. One reason that Akiva represents the very embodiment of the rabbinic world is that he is at the center of this world of debate and disputation. The relationship between Akiva and Eliezer ben Hyrcanus highlights the complexities of these connections. The midrashic text Song of Songs Rabbah relates the following story:

> One day Rabbi Akiva came late to the Beit Midrash and he sat outdoors. A question was asked about a particular matter:

"Is this the law?" They said, "The law is outside." Again a question arose, and they said: "The Torah is outside." Again a question arose, and they said, "Akiva is outside—make room for him." He came and sat at the feet of Rabbi Eliezer.

Song of Songs Rabbah 1:20

As I described in chapter 1, most scholars today believe that the institution of the Beit Midrash, which may look in this story like a formal "academy," did not yet exist in Akiva's lifetime, and it appears that Song of Songs Rabbah projects back in time the institution that later became the center of rabbinic society.[7] That being said, the actual historical context does not affect the thrust of the story. It seems that Akiva, like a college student who has overslept his morning class, chose to sit outside because the session had already begun. But perhaps there is something else going on as well. Could it be that Akiva chooses not to interrupt specifically because it is Rabbi Eliezer who is teaching? Indeed, one is tempted to put this story together with a remarkable moment reported in the Jerusalem Talmud. There we read of a debate between Eliezer and Akiva about the issue of whether Sabbath restrictions can be overridden to allow for preparing the special sacrifice done on Passover. Akiva disagrees with Eliezer's position and wins the debate. The text then adds the following details:

For thirteen years Rabbi Akiva would come before Rabbi Eliezer and Rabbi Eliezer did not pay any attention to him. And this statement [about Sabbath restrictions and the paschal sacrifice] by Akiva comprised the opening of his first response before Rabbi Eliezer.

Rabbi Joshua, applying a biblical verse in appreciation of Akiva, said to Rabbi Eliezer, "*There* is the army you sneered at; now go out and fight it" (Judges 9:38).

y. Pesahim "Passover" 6:3[8]

93

We learn from this story that Rabbi Eliezer essentially ignored Akiva for a period of years. Of course, we should take the "thirteen years" as a poetic hyperbole, but the point is clear: for whatever reason, Eliezer paid no attention to Akiva until the moment in which Akiva outdid him in rabbinic argument. Rabbi Joshua's clever use of the verse from Judges sums it up well: you didn't pay him any heed, and now he has come and defeated you.

Once again, it is the relationship with Joshua that seems to be the close one for Akiva. If we circle back to the story of Akiva standing outside after coming late to class, we can understand his hesitancy at entering the room. His relationship with Eliezer was problematic, and interrupting that particular teacher in the middle of his discourse might well have seemed impossible to Akiva.

While Eliezer may have ignored Akiva, Akiva's fellow students had come to understand the power of his intelligence and insight. In our story, structured in the three-part model of a good moral tale or a classic joke, first a question of law is asked. We don't know who asks the question, but I think it's fair to assume that it comes from the teacher, Rabbi Eliezer. The students can't answer the question but say instead, "The law is outside." Second, another kind of question is asked (one assumes from the students' response that in this case it is a matter of non-legal interpretation of Torah). "The Torah is outside," they all say. Finally a third question is asked and the students respond, "Akiva is outside—make room for him." Of course the answer in each of the three parts of the story is the same: "Akiva." The law is Akiva; the Torah is Akiva; the answer is Akiva. Note that they don't say, "Akiva knows the answer." They say, Akiva *is* the answer. "Why should we be worrying about these questions," the students seem to be saying, "when the very *embodiment* of the answers stands outside?"

Rabbi Eliezer cannot be pleased.

Yet Akiva comes in and "sat at the feet of Rabbi Eliezer." This gesture reminds us of Rachel kissing Akiva's feet upon his return home and Kalba Savua making the same gesture. Here Akiva *sits* at Eliezer's feet, but we are left to wonder whether it is a gesture of respect or perhaps one of resigned submission.

The tension between Eliezer and Akiva, teacher and student, appears in a variety of places in rabbinic literature. In the tractate on Passover in the Babylonian Talmud the discussion of the rules governing the Passover sacrifice and the restrictions of the Sabbath are debated in a fashion similar to what we saw above in the passage from the Jerusalem Talmud. But in the midst of this debate a strange interchange happens. Akiva has outwitted Eliezer in the discussion, and Eliezer turns to him with these ominous words: "Akiva, you have refuted me in the discussion about the ritual slaughter of sacrifices—by slaughter shall be his death!" (Pesahim 69a). The switch from second-person address ("you have refuted me") to third person ("his death") makes it seem that in the second half of his words, Eliezer is not so much speaking to Akiva as he is making a public prediction about Akiva's violent death, something of course that will occur. In other words, it sounds a good deal more like a curse than a point made by a conversant in a dialogue. This interpretation is supported, I believe, by the way that Akiva reacts to Eliezer's words, saying in essence, "Don't be angry with me—I'm only repeating a teaching I learned from you!" In typical fashion the Talmud goes on to have another rabbi try to show that in fact Eliezer and Akiva were really *not* disagreeing with one another in the point of law, but rather each of them was speaking about a different specific case and not a general principle. It feels like an unconvincing attempt to minimize the conflict between the two disputants.

But soon after in the same discussion a more interesting interpretation of the differences between Eliezer and Akiva is raised: "Since Rabbi Eliezer himself had taught it to Rabbi Akiva,

what is the reason that Rabbi Eliezer took the opposite position in this argument?" That is, why is Eliezer disagreeing with
his own view, which was simply repeated back to him by Akiva?
The Talmud then answers its own question: "Rabbi Eliezer had
forgotten his own tradition and Rabbi Akiva came to remind
him of that tradition." "In that case," the anonymous editorial
voice of the Talmud asks, "why didn't Akiva tell Eliezer directly
that he was only quoting Eliezer's own tradition?" The answer?
"Rabbi Akiva thought that it would not be proper behavior" to
point that out to Rabbi Eliezer.

A good deal of ambiguity resides in this short passage. Is it
really possible that Eliezer had forgotten his own previous position on the matter being debated? And if so—as Akiva himself
seems to be arguing—perhaps this passage is meant to emphasize Eliezer's weakness, his faltering memory, in contrast to his
brilliant and combative student Akiva. As we have seen, one
theme that repeats itself in the stories about Akiva and Eliezer
is the changing tide of intellectual and moral authority within
the burgeoning rabbinic world. Akiva is becoming the dominant
voice. Immediately before the passage in the Jerusalem Talmud
quoted above, Eliezer uses a classic rabbinic style of argumentation to try to win a point in his dispute over the law with Akiva.
But Akiva takes the very same argument and says back to Eliezer:
one could take your words and use them to make exactly the
opposite point. Eliezer is incensed; "Akiva," he says, "you are
uprooting the Torah!" And yet, as the Mishnah tells us, the law
follows Akiva's ruling. The student does uproot the teacher.

When our story says that Akiva keeps quiet out of polite-
ness or a sense of what is "good behavior," I am not convinced.
More plausible is a reading of the story as it appears on the
page: Akiva is perfectly happy to take on his teacher and repay
thirteen years of being ignored with a winning attack that actually quotes Eliezer back at himself. The world of the rabbis has
its cruelties.

One further story about the tension between Eliezer and Akiva may offer us a different angle. In the Babylonian Talmud tractate Ta'anit ("Fast Days") we read a tale in which the issue is a matter of life and death: What can be done to overcome a drought? In the ancient world, particularly in the Middle East, rainfall was a crucial factor in the day-to-day lives of the community. Fasts were proclaimed to try to influence divine favor, and special prayers were offered:

> Once it happened during a drought that Rabbi Eliezer stood before the congregation and recited the twenty-four special prayers for a fast day. His prayer was not answered.
>
> Rabbi Akiva stood before the congregation after him and prayed: "Our Father, our King, we have no King but You; our Father, our King, for Your sake have mercy upon us."[9] And rains fell.
>
> The rabbis murmured about Rabbi Eliezer, at which point a heavenly voice was heard saying: "It is not because this man is greater than that man that caused one prayer to be answered and the other not. Rather it is because this man [Rabbi Akiva] is a forgiving person and the other is not."
>
> b. Ta'anit 25b

The rabbis "murmured": this is a way of saying that they gossiped about the lack of divine favor shown to Rabbi Eliezer. His star is fading. But a voice from heaven offers an alternative view, telling them that the different results from the two prayers reflect the different *personal qualities* of the two rabbis. Akiva is "forgiving"; Eliezer is not. What does the text mean by a "forgiving person"? Perhaps the intention here is to mean being forgiving of other people's foibles, not retaliating for wrongs that have been done to you. In one case in the Talmud the same Hebrew phrase is used in the context of not holding a grudge. In several other places one rabbi is quoted as saying that a person who has the quality of "forgiving" alone is in turn forgiven for all of his sins on Yom Kippur. To be forgiving, to forget past insults and hurts—is that what Rabbi Eliezer is lacking? Is that the quality that Akiva has?

Akiva can be tough-minded; he can hold unbendingly to opinions, but the quality of letting go, of forgiving the past, may be what separates him from Rabbi Eliezer. At least that is the heavenly judgment in the text from Tractate Ta'anit when it explains why Akiva's prayer is answered while Eliezer's is not. And it is this quality of not forgiving old insults that we will see in the sad, indeed tragic, conclusion to Eliezer's story (see chapter 5).

Perhaps also Akiva's forgiving nature is one reason that his colleagues hold him in such high regard. Yes, he is star of the classroom; he is the "Torah" itself, sitting outside the room waiting to be invited in. But he is also sensitive to the needs of his community. Alongside his brilliance, he has an extraordinarily spiritual nature as well. We will see this in more detail when we look at the mystical side of Akiva (chapter 6), but as one small example, consider the following story of the way that Akiva bridges his exceptionalism with the demands of community:

> Our rabbis taught: when a person prays, he should direct his heart toward heaven. . . . It has been taught: such was the custom of Rabbi Akiva—when he prayed with the congregation, he used to shorten his prayers in order not to be a burden on the congregation. But when he prayed by himself, a person would leave Akiva standing in one corner and find him later in another corner, because of how much he bowed and moved during prayer.
>
> b. Berakhot 31a

This text comes in the midst of an extended talmudic discussion about the meaning and importance of intentionality and focus during prayer and the performance of the commandments, a concept known as *kavannah* in Hebrew, literally, "direction." Akiva is an example of a person who has attained an extraordinary degree of *kavannah* in his devotional life. He is so focused that he does not even realize how he has moved from one side of the room to the other while he has been "directing his heart toward heaven." But this story serves another purpose as well: Akiva is a man who has an equally deep concern for his community. Despite the fact that he outstrips them in the concentration he brings to prayer, he nonetheless cuts his own prayers short when he is praying with others so as not to inconvenience them and, I think, not *embarrass* them by outdoing them in prayer. In other words, despite the brilliance that he shows in intellectual debate, there is a deep modesty in Akiva that accompanies his special gifts.

But Akiva's modesty and connection to his fellows are not limited to the realm of the spiritual, as we see in the following text from the early midrashic text Sifre Deuteronomy (chapter 1):

> Rabbi Tarfon said: I swear by the Temple service, I wonder if there is anyone in this generation who is able to give rebuke to another. Rabbi Eleazar ben Azariah said: I swear by the Temple service I wonder if there is anyone in this generation who is able to *receive* rebuke from another. Rabbi Akiva said: I swear by the Temple service I wonder if there is anyone in this generation who knows *how* one should give rebuke to another.
>
> Rabbi Yohanan ben Nuri said: I call heaven and earth to witness for me that Rabbi Akiva was rebuked because of me more than five times before Rabban Gamaliel in Yavneh. I used to complain about Akiva, and Rabban Gamaliel would rebuke him. But I truly know that each time Akiva was rebuked, he loved me more and more. For it says in scripture: "Do not rebuke a scoffer, for he will hate you. Rebuke a wise man and he will love you" (Proverbs 9:8).

One of the most interesting ethical questions that rabbinic literature deals with is the importance of rebuking your neighbor when you believe a wrong has been done—either to you personally or to the community as a whole. This concept of rebuke has its origins in the Bible itself; in fact, the principle is announced preceding one of the most recognizable lines in the entire Bible, indeed in all of Western culture:

> You shall not hate your brother in your heart. You shall surely rebuke your neighbor but bear no sin because of him. You shall not take vengeance nor bear a grudge against your countrymen. Love your neighbor as yourself: I am the Lord.
>
> Leviticus 19:17–18

These few sentences, appearing in two verses in the Hebrew Bible, have occasioned centuries of debate and discussion. What is the relationship between the "love your neighbor" part and that which goes before it? What does rebuking without "bearing sin" mean?

In the story from Sifre Deuteronomy we have four characters. First, Rabbi Tarfon argues that, as important as rebuke is, we live in a time when it is highly unlikely for anyone to actually rebuke another. The text here is somewhat opaque about why that might be the case, but a parallel version of this discussion in the Babylonian Talmud makes it clear. If you rebuke someone else, the other person is very likely to reply with an even greater rebuke to you (b. Arakhin "Temple Vows" 16b).

Second, Rabbi Eleazar ben Azariah suggests that the real problem is that no one knows how to *receive* rebuke. Rather than lashing out, as the Talmud describes it, or getting defensive and argumentative, no one knows how to listen to rebuke, accept it, and learn from it. Third, Akiva adds a different perspective. The real problem, he suggests, is that no one understands the best way to rebuke another person. If the person doing the rebuking understood *how* to rebuke, rebuke would be more easily accepted by the other.

Here is another example of the pattern in a discussion in

which three opinions are voiced, with Akiva's being the final one in the group; this seems to suggest that his idea is the answer we should embrace. Of course, it's perfectly reasonable in this case to argue that the debate articulates three equally viable responses to the problematics of rebuke. Each has its own validity. But the notion that the answer rests with Akiva is strengthened here by the coda to our story, the rather striking remarks of the fourth character in our drama, Rabbi Yohanan ben Nuri.

Yohanan gives us another glimpse into the world of rabbinic debate. It appears, according to this story, that Yohanan used to complain to Rabban Gamaliel about Akiva, and this led to Akiva's being rebuked by his teacher. But Rabbi Yohanan adds, "Each time Akiva was rebuked, he loved me more and more." Why was that so? Yohanan brings a proof text from Proverbs in which we learn that the wise person who is criticized learns from that criticism and sees it as an occasion for self-improvement.

The story of Rabbi Yohanan ben Nuri leaves out some important details. What was it about Akiva that led Yohanan to complain to Rabban Gamaliel when the two of them were Gamaliel's students? We are given no clue, but it is not hard to imagine that the intellectual star quality of Akiva may have made him a difficult colleague in class. But clearly what Akiva did have was the quality of wisdom extolled by Proverbs; Akiva was able to learn from his mistakes, and in this story once again we see those two attractive aspects of his character. It is Akiva who worries about the right way to critique another with sensitivity, and it is Akiva who knows how to accept rebuke. He doesn't lash out at Yohanan; instead, his love for Yohanan grows —not *despite* the complaints and criticism, but *because* of them. Akiva understood what it meant to grow through difficult experiences. Indeed, Yohanan ben Nuri's comment encourages us to recall the rebuke Akiva received from Rabbi Eliezer and

Rabbi Joshua about carrying the dead body for burial. There we saw Akiva's reaction to rebuke: he didn't sulk, he didn't react in anger; instead, he took upon himself the best path to his own development, namely, "serving the sages." And through that, he became a sage himself.

One final word about Akiva and his teachers. A midrashic text reports the following reflections of Rabbi Eliezer, Rabbi Joshua, and Rabbi Akiva about the nature of learning Torah:

> Rabbi Eliezer said: If all the seas were ink and all the reeds were pens and the heaven and earth were scrolls, and all human beings were scribes, they would not suffice to write all the Torah that I have learned, and yet I took no more from it than a man would take by dipping the point of a paintbrush into the sea.
>
> Rabbi Joshua said: If all the seas were ink and all the reeds were pens and the heaven and earth were writing sheets, and all human beings were scribes, they would not suffice to write all the words of Torah that I have learned, and yet I took no more from it than a man would take by dipping the point of a paintbrush into the sea.
>
> Rabbi Akiva said: I am not able to say what my two masters have said for in fact my masters *did* take something from their study of Torah—while I have taken no more than one who smells a citron: he who smells enjoys it, while nothing is taken away from the citron. Or I am like one who fills a pitcher from flowing water, or one who lights one lamp from another.

Song of Songs Rabbah 1:20

In virtually the same words Akiva's two main teachers speak about what they have learned from Torah and how much of Torah still remains untapped. One could not possibly write down all that one learned, both of them say; and yet in the great scheme of things, they are like one who dips the very tip of a paintbrush into the sea, extracting hardly a drop of its water.

Eliezer and Joshua are not boasting about how much they have learned; rather, they are overwhelmed by how much of Torah is still left to be explored.

Akiva's words are at once an expression of his modesty and his admiration for his two teachers. As much as we have seen his complicated and often contested relationship with Rabbi Eliezer (less so with Rabbi Joshua), the text here shows his appreciation for how much he has learned from both men. Is this only a *show* of modesty? Does Akiva really believe that while they have managed to extract something from Torah, he has not even touched its surface? Akiva uses three metaphors to express this idea: he is like a person who has smelled a fragrant fruit, the citron (*etrog* in Hebrew—the fruit that is part of the ritual associated with the fall harvest festival of Sukkot); he is like a person who fills a pitcher from a powerful stream of water; and he is like one who lights a lamp from another lamp. In each case the actions of the person involved do not in any way diminish the object—the citron, the stream, the lamp all remain as they were. Do Eliezer and Joshua believe that they have *lessened* Torah? I don't think that is their intention, but they have taken something from it. The bigger question for our purposes is, What does Akiva really think about his accomplishments in relation to his two masters? Certainly throughout the stories about his life, we see both sides of him: he is a man with enormous self-confidence, and yet at the same time a person of great humility. From these words alone we cannot really know what he is thinking.

And yet perhaps beneath the surface something is being communicated to us here—not so much by Akiva's words as by the ancient editors of Song of Songs Rabbah. Those editors placed the text quoted above immediately before the story we looked at earlier about Akiva sitting outside the classroom and eventually being called into the room to address the questions the other students could not answer. Why would the editors have made this choice? It is, I believe, the editors' response to Akiva's statement of modesty: yes, he may have seen himself as merely smelling the fragrance of the *etrog*, but *we*—say the editors—know better. Akiva is the representative of Torah learning at its highest. So his fellow students understand it, and so eventually will the rest of the Jewish world.

The rise of Akiva may be the story that we are seeing here, but it certainly does not mean that he wins every argument. In fact, such an outcome would fly in the face of rabbinic culture. In that culture, some were teachers and some were students—there were masters and disciples—but this was a society in which all the rabbis were constantly being both students and teachers at the same time.

It was an intellectual meritocracy, despite some obvious and complicating differences in social and financial status. There was no course of study, no "curriculum" in the modern sense of the word, that one followed to become a rabbi. There was no graduation ceremony with caps and gowns. Because of that and because, as I have said, we do not have clear chronological biographies within rabbinic literature, we can only surmise that at some point Akiva stopped "serving the sages" and became one himself. Nonetheless, the rest of his life was bound up with those same figures who were his teachers, colleagues, and students.

It appears that the rabbis traveled a good deal from place to place, but at least some of them became associated with one particular locality above others—for example, Rabban Gamaliel with Yavneh and Rabbi Eliezer ben Hyrcanus with Lod. Akiva is connected to the city Bene-Berak (not far from Jaffa), although the evidence for his settling there is not as robust as one might have thought. The Babylonian Talmud tractate Sanhedrin ("Law Court" 32b) includes a short list of the places where various rabbis settled, and Akiva is said to have gone to Bene-Berak.

And, most famously, there is the story that appears early in the annual Passover Seder that tells about the all-night discussion of the Exodus from Egypt—a conversation that took place in Bene-Berak among Akiva, Rabbi Eliezer, Rabbi Joshua, Rabbi Eleazar ben Azariah, and Rabbi Tarfon. These rabbis were so involved in their discussion that it continued until sunrise and they had to be interrupted by their students so they could proceed to the morning prayers before it got too late.

Yet despite the association of Akiva with Bene-Berak, it is clear from our sources that there was an almost constant interchange and geographic movement among the small group of sages. How accurate this is historically, of course, we have no way of knowing. But in the way the stories are told, we see all these rabbis engaged in ongoing debate, disagreement, and intellectual conflict. Indeed, this was a culture in which conflict was likely to be a constant companion. Some of the most monumental crises and struggles in the early stages of Judaism involved Akiva and his peers. And at the same time it was a tightly knit society of enormous support, vision, and spiritual power. We now turn to stories about this community of scholars.

5

Among the Rabbis

As I HAVE SAID, we do not know—and cannot know—the
year-by-year history of Akiva's life, but it is clear that the classic
sources present him as a person whom his fellow students admired, both as a scholar and as a human being, and his reputation continued to grow as he left his years of preparation and
became a rabbinic figure in his own right. The Babylonian Talmud tells a story about a number of rabbis wishing to consult
with Rabbi Dosa ben Harkinas, one of the last sages alive from
the first generation of rabbinic scholars. The rabbis believe that
they are about to overturn one of Dosa's rulings, and before
doing so, they want to tell him about their decision and gauge
his reaction. Three rabbis are appointed to meet with him:
Rabbi Joshua, Rabbi Eleazar ben Azariah, and Rabbi Akiva.

Dosa ben Harkinas greets each of them as they enter his
room. Akiva is the last to enter, and when he comes into the
room, Rabbi Dosa exclaims:

"Are you Akiva son of Joseph whose name is known from one end of the world to the other? Sit down, my son, sit down. May those like you multiply in Israel."

b. Yevamot "Levirate Marriage" 16b

To this elderly figure, a contemporary of Rabban Yohanan ben Zakkai, Akiva's presence is an extraordinary event. And Dosa gives Akiva his blessing, viewing him as a model for all Jews.

Interestingly, a few lines later the story describes Akiva's encounter in the next room with Rabbi Dosa's contentious and trouble-making younger brother, Jonathan. When Jonathan greets Akiva, Jonathan insults him, mimicking his older brother's words but in a disparaging way:

"Are you Akiva whose name is known from one end of the world to the other? You are blessed indeed to have won fame even though you have not yet attained the rank of ox herders." "Not even," replied Rabbi Akiva, "that of shepherds."

Jonathan mocks Akiva—essentially saying, "Amazing that you have attained such fame, since you are hardly at the level of the lowliest of farmworkers!" Akiva's response to Jonathan is typical of what we have seen in Akiva before. He is quick to forgive, and even an egregious insult elicits only an expression of Akiva's humility. We can wonder, of course, whether Akiva really views himself as so unexceptional, but at the very least he responds to belligerence with modesty.

The story of Akiva and the visit to Rabbi Dosa ben Harkinas is only one example of the status Akiva has attained among the other sages, and that status is embedded in the structure of the story. We have seen this pattern before, and it is repeated in numerous examples in the rabbinic corpus: there is a discussion (or, as in this case, an event—the visit to Dosa) that involves three rabbis. Two opinions are voiced; then Akiva's view is stated last, capping the argument. Akiva often has, as it were, the last word.

In the Passover Haggadah, for example, there is a discussion of the ten plagues brought upon the Egyptians before the Exodus.[1] Three rabbis—Yose the Galilean, Eliezer, and Akiva—use their skills of midrashic interpretation to deduce that as terrible as the plagues might have been, the Egyptians were visited by many more plagues as they pursued the Israelites crossing through the Sea of Reeds (the "Red Sea" in earlier translations). Rabbi Yose claims that he can interpret the biblical verse "and the magicians [of Egypt] said to Pharaoh, 'It is the finger of God'" (Exodus 8:15) by reading it in relationship to the later verse describing the scene at the sea: "And Israel saw the great hand which the Lord laid upon the Egyptians" (Exodus 14:31). Yose's inventive, perhaps even playful, interpretation calculates by midrashic "mathematics" that if ten plagues were caused by the *finger* of God, then the *hand* of God at the sea would account for fifty plagues (five fingers times ten plagues for each finger equals fifty plagues).

Not to be outdone, Rabbi Eliezer takes the discussion even further. He offers a verse from Psalms to show that each plague in Egypt could be multiplied by four in terms of its force and horror. Using Rabbi Yose's mathematical method in a more complex way, Eliezer concludes that at the sea the *hand* of God would mean that the Egyptians' suffering was equal to two hundred plagues (four times fifty).

The discussion concludes with Rabbi Akiva. He follows Eliezer's logic but takes it another step: there really were *five*, not four, dimensions of power in each plague: five plagues for each finger and five fingers on the hand of God at the sea—hence the Egyptians experienced 250 plagues at the sea (five times fifty).

The "logic" of the midrash is anything but clear to a modern sensibility. Indeed, it is hard to know why this midrash is presented here, aside from its obvious connection to the story of the Exodus. But for our purposes, this text is yet another—

and quite obvious—example of the familiar trope we could call (in the spirit of the text we looked at in the last chapter) "Akiva is the Torah." Even in a kind of mathematical competition Akiva wins; his 250 plagues outdoes the numbers of his two colleagues. This text, in possibly a humorous fashion, once again confirms Akiva's status and importance, but underneath it is something else as well. As we will see, one of the defining characteristics of Akiva, one of his monumental contributions to Jewish religious history, is his dedication to the principle that interpretation of Torah requires paying careful attention to every detail in the text. That kind of close reading in all its subtlety and all its elements becomes the hallmark of Jewish interpretation for millennia to come. And even here in a comical (perhaps even a parodic) way, we see Akiva's interpretive creativity.

We find Akiva appearing in some of the most famous and important stories about the sages recounted in rabbinic literature. At times he is an onlooker, not the central figure in the events described; but even in those cases, he invariably appears in a significant moment or role.

We now turn to two of the most well-known stories in the rabbinic canon to see Akiva amidst the world of the sages. Once again, we must remember that these stories appear in sources composed many years after the setting of the tales. We should not be looking at them as historically accurate accounts of events but rather as literary representations of crucial issues in the life of rabbinic culture. And for that culture perhaps no issue is more compelling or troubling than that of the nature of authority. Akiva and his colleagues were deeply concerned with questions such as, Who is a leader? Who has power? How diffused is authority? In whose hands does tradition lie? Questions of this sort haunt many of these cornerstone tales in the emerging years of Judaism as it was coming to be defined. Akiva is part of virtually all of them.

One of the most elaborate of these tales—about the revolt

against the leadership of the Patriarch Rabban Gamaliel II—is recounted in the Mishnah and expanded upon in both the Jerusalem Talmud and the Babylonian Talmud. According to rabbinic lore Rabban Gamaliel, as we have seen, was a descendent of an illustrious line of leaders dating back to Hillel the Elder. Rabbinic sources present Gamaliel II as ruling with an iron hand. On three occasions we see him wielding his power over Akiva's teacher Rabbi Joshua in disputes in which Joshua took a different position from Gamaliel's. One case—a somewhat obscure matter for us today—dealt with judging whether a blemished animal was fit for use as a sacrifice. Another case focused on the important matter of determining the calendar. In the lunar calendar of Jewish tradition the new month began with the appearance of the new moon; at a time before the mathematical calculation of the calendar, witnesses were needed to testify that they had actually seen the new moon so that the date could be officially fixed and announced. Since Jewish festivals are located according to their date within a particular month, figuring out the start of any given month had crucial consequences for the festivals and fast days of the ritual year.

The Mishnah recounts an episode in which Rabbi Joshua and Rabban Gamaliel disagreed about the reliability of certain witnesses who reported seeing the new moon marking the start of the Hebrew month of Tishrei. Tishrei is a particularly important month in the Jewish calendar since it includes Rosh Hashanah (the new year), Yom Kippur (the "day of atonement"), and the harvest festival of Sukkot. Gamaliel declared that Joshua was wrong and, driving his point home, insisted: "I order you to appear before me with your staff and your money on the day which according to *your* calculation should be Yom Kippur," the holiest day of the Jewish year (m. Rosh Hashanah 2:9). In other words, Gamaliel was making Joshua violate a core stricture forbidding carrying objects and using money on Yom Kippur. Joshua was being made to publicly accept Gamaliel's determination that that day was *not* Yom Kippur even though according to Joshua's reckoning it *was* the sacred day. Gamaliel did more than disagree or overrule Joshua; he aimed to humiliate him in public and make him violate his personal principles by disgracing Yom Kippur.

At this point Akiva comes into the story in a small but significant way:

> Rabbi Akiva went and found him [Joshua] in distress. Akiva said to him, "I can teach you that whatever Rabban Gamaliel has done is correct: it says in the Torah 'These are the fixed times [that is, the festivals] of the Lord, holy times. You shall proclaim them as sacred times' (Leviticus 23:4). Whether they are proclaimed at their proper time or not at their proper time, I have no other festivals except for these."

> m. Rosh Hashanah 2:9

After Joshua's humiliation by Gamaliel, Akiva seeks out his teacher to offer comfort. The dispute with Gamaliel revolved around the calculation of the calendar, and Akiva's method shows Joshua that it would be possible for Joshua to accept Gamaliel's ruling about the date and to appear on the day that Joshua believed to be Yom Kippur carrying his staff and his money.

Akiva begins by quoting a fairly straightforward verse from Leviticus about the proclamation of festivals. Is there, Akiva asks, an eternal, ideal calendar? Or is the calendar essentially a human construct? The verse in Akiva's reading would emphasize the clause "you shall proclaim them" from the quoted verse— with emphasis on the word "you." In other words, human beings make the calendar, and human beings proclaim the festivals, even though the calendar is based on events in nature (the appearance of the new moon) over which humans have no control. The date of Yom Kippur? Even if the authorities get it "wrong" in an absolute, astronomical way (misreading the new moon's appearance), it doesn't matter. The case is determined by human agency. Akiva is saying that by bowing to the will of authority as represented by the Patriarch, Joshua would not be compromising his principles and violating Yom Kippur; he would be acknowledging the fact that human courts decide the calendar and Joshua has simply been outvoted.

It is typical of Akiva that he comforts Joshua through the use of text interpretation. Rabbi Joshua is, after all, Akiva's main teacher, and it is perhaps an appropriate insight to try to help Joshua by becoming *his* teacher at this moment. Akiva thinks that it is precisely this kind of answer that will please Joshua and bring him comfort.

Joshua then seeks other advice, turning to the elderly Rabbi Dosa ben Harkinas. Dosa also urges Joshua to bow to Gamaliel's ruling. Dosa says to Joshua: if you question this decision, you are undermining *all* authority of every court in Jewish history. In essence he asks, "Do you wish to bring down the entire system?"

Finally, Joshua relents—perhaps because of the combination of Akiva's and Dosa's words. Perhaps he has just grown weary of fighting. But at any rate the next lines of our Mishnah give us the dénouement: "He took his staff and his money and went to Yavneh, to Rabban Gamaliel on the day that according to Joshua's count should have been Yom Kippur." Clearly, Gamaliel has won; he has established the authority of the court, and for the sake of unity and communal polity the decision may have been the right one. But in doing so he has hurt and humiliated Joshua, and as we will see, the rest of the sages long remember these events.

These are the events as reported in the Mishnah, a text that was composed around one hundred years after the death of Gamaliel. Interestingly, the Babylonian Talmud—a text composed almost five hundred years after the Mishnah[2]—expands on the story of Akiva's comforting, deepening our understanding of his empathy. The passage begins with a quotation from the Mishnah we have been reading, "Rabbi Akiva went and found Rabbi Joshua in distress" and then continues:

> Rabbi Akiva said to him, "Master, why are you in distress?"
>
> Rabbi Joshua replied: "Akiva, it would be better for me to be on a sickbed for twelve months than that such an injunction should be put upon me."
>
> Rabbi Akiva said to him, "Will you allow me to tell you something that you yourself have taught me?"
>
> Rabbi Joshua said to him, "Speak."
>
> Rabbi Akiva then said to him: "The text says, 'you,' three times [in three separate verses], to indicate that 'you' may fix the date of the festivals even if you err inadvertently; 'you,' even if you err deliberately; 'you,' even if you are misled."
>
> Rabbi Joshua replied to him in these words: "Akiva, you have comforted me, you have comforted me."
>
> b. Rosh Hashanah 25a

Retellings of stories about Akiva in the Babylonian Talmud tend to deepen or expand his role and status, as we see here in the way the Talmud presents the Mishnah's original story. In this narrative the text adds an interesting detail. Akiva says to Joshua, "Will you allow me to tell you something that you yourself have taught me?" We have seen this move before—students telling their teachers or former teachers that they are only repeating something they had previously learned from those very teachers. In the case that I recounted in chapter 4, Akiva used this phrase to defeat Rabbi Eliezer in a dispute about the Passover sacrifice and the rules of the Sabbath. In that story Akiva's words were either defensive and apologetic or aggressively triumphant, depending on how we read the encounter. But here the words are clearly meant to be of comfort to the rabbi in distress. By quoting Joshua's teaching back to Joshua, Akiva means to say: "You should not feel upset because you yourself have taught us that the determination of the dates is truly in human hands. If Gamaliel's court has determined the date of Yom Kippur differently from your calculation, you can accept his ruling."

In the Mishnah's version of the story, as we've seen, Akiva uses a verse from Leviticus to help comfort Joshua. Here in the Babylonian Talmud's telling he uses a different interpretative strategy. Instead of honing in on a single verse from Leviticus, he alludes to that verse (Leviticus 23:4) along with two others, Leviticus 22:31 ("You shall observe my commandments and do them") and Leviticus 23:2 ("These are my fixed times, the fixed times of the Lord. You shall proclaim them as sacred times").

The Hebrew word for "them" (*otam*), which appears in all three verses, almost precisely resembles the Hebrew word for "you" in the plural (*atem*). Akiva plays on that resemblance to emphasize the fact that a group of human beings (here he alludes to Gamaliel's court) has the right to declare when the festivals ("the fixed times," in biblical language) can be celebrated. By hearing his own words quoted back to him, Rabbi Joshua is assuaged: "You have comforted me, Akiva, you have comforted me."

Both Akiva's interpretive creativity and his human compassion are emphasized in this telling of the story. Indeed, the Babylonian Talmud has magnified his role—perhaps because his importance in the rabbinic imagination had grown so significantly by the time of the Talmud's composition. But the extended story of Rabbi Joshua and Rabban Gamaliel does not end here. There is one more humiliation for Joshua and finally a reaction by the rabbinic community as a whole.

This case, once again told in the Mishnah, centers on a question about whether the evening prayer service was mandatory or optional. For traditional Jews today, the evening service (called *Arvit* or *Ma'ariv*) is obligatory, but in ancient times this was still a matter of some debate. Rabbinic tradition linked the daily mandatory prayer services to the sacrifices that had been

offered in the Temple before its destruction. Sacrifices were offered daily in the morning and the afternoon, but there was no
separate evening sacrifice. With the destruction of the Temple,
Jews came to view prayer as a substitute for the sacrificial cult,[3]
hence the question of the evening service as a requirement was
an open one in the early Rabbinic Period: since there had been
no evening sacrifice in the Temple, was an evening prayer service obligatory or merely a matter of choice? The Babylonian
Talmud relates the following incident in connection to this
question:

> A certain student came before Rabbi Joshua and asked him,
> "Is the evening prayer compulsory or optional?"
> Rabbi Joshua replied: "It is optional."
> The same student then came before Rabban Gamaliel and
> asked him: "Is the evening prayer compulsory or optional?"
> Rabban Gamaliel replied: "It is compulsory."
> "But," the student said, "didn't Rabbi Joshua tell me
> that it is optional?"
> Rabban Gamaliel said: "Wait till the 'shield-bearers'
> enter the Beit Midrash." When the 'shield-bearers' came in,
> the same questioner stood up and asked, "Is the evening
> prayer compulsory or optional?" Rabban Gamaliel replied:
> "It is compulsory."
> Rabban Gamaliel said to the sages: "Is there anyone
> who disagrees with me about this matter?" R. Joshua replied
> to him: "No."
> Rabban Gamaliel said to him: "But wasn't I told in your
> name that you said it was optional?" He then went on:
> "Joshua, get up on your feet and let them testify against you!"
> Rabbi Joshua stood up and said: "If I were alive and he
> [the student who asked the question] were dead, the living
> could contradict the dead. But now since he is alive and I am
> alive, how can the living contradict the living?"
> Rabban Gamaliel remained sitting and teaching while
> Rabbi Joshua remained standing, until all the people began

to complain and said to Hutzpit the *turgeman*:[4] "Stop!" And Hutzpit stopped.

They then said: "How long is Rabban Gamaliel to go on causing pain to Rabbi Joshua? On Rosh Hashanah last year he caused him pain. He did the same in the matter of the blemished animal being fit for sacrifice. And now he causes pain to him again! Come, let us depose him!"

b. Berakhot "Blessings" 27b

Note Rabban Gamaliel's use of the term "shield-bearers" as an epithet for "the sages." The idea that the Beit Midrash is a place of conflict and intellectual violence is well-expressed by this military metaphor. And it becomes more apt than Gamaliel realizes when his behavior leads to a full-scale revolt by the rest of the rabbis. The pain being caused to Rabbi Joshua through a series of public humiliations orchestrated by Rabban Gamaliel reaches a breaking point here. The sages remember the two prior incidents, and now that a third has occurred, they have reached the limit of their tolerance for their leader's authoritarian manner of control.

We can wonder, as well, about Rabbi Joshua's behavior in this story. When Gamaliel asks whether anyone disagrees with his ruling, Joshua lacks the courage of his convictions and will not disagree with Gamaliel. It's interesting that Joshua is the only voice recorded in our story. At least in the way that this tale has come down to us, none of the other rabbis speaks up, even in support of Gamaliel.

We clearly see the artistry of the storyteller at play here. We might speculate how this might be portrayed in a play or film: Does Rabban Gamaliel look directly at Rabbi Joshua when he asks, "Is there anyone who disagrees with me about this matter"? Or perhaps Joshua, worried that his previous opinion on the question will become known to Gamaliel, guiltily blurts out his response "No" before any of the other rabbis has a chance to speak. As a subtle literary piece the text is morally ambiguous: Gamaliel, knowing quite well how Joshua answered the student's original question about the evening prayer, seems to be cruelly baiting Joshua by asking whether anyone disagrees with him. Joshua seems less than admirable in his saying that if there were not a living witness to testify to what he previously said in answer to the student's question, essentially he could have lied about it. And even the student who asked the original question is an ambiguous figure: Why did he make a point of "informing" on Rabbi Joshua to Rabban Gamaliel? Was he merely an innocent seeking clarification, or is he somehow stirring up trouble for purposes of his own?

The story is painted in shades of gray, not in clear strokes of black and white; nonetheless, the moral weight of the narrative leans heavily against Rabban Gamaliel. The sages' outrage about his conduct in regard to Rabbi Joshua gains the sympathy of the reader, and in the way that the narrator tells the tale, we are on the side of the revolt.

The story is working hard at balancing two tensions embedded deeply in rabbinic culture—tensions that will endure throughout later Jewish history. On the one hand, there is a need for a reliable, ongoing continuity of decision-making and tradition. On the other hand, there is a deeply held desire to acknowledge and valorize challenges to that tradition—what some scholars have called the "multivocality" or "legal pluralism" of Jewish tradition, meaning many voices can be heard.

The deposing of Rabban Gamaliel is not, indeed cannot be, the end of this story. What leadership will come in his place? The Talmud continues:

> Whom shall we raise up instead? We cannot raise up Rabbi Joshua because he is one of the parties involved. We cannot raise up Rabbi Akiva—perhaps Rabban Gamaliel will harm him because Akiva has no ancestral merit. Rather let us raise up Rabbi Eleazar ben Azariah, who is wise and rich and the

tenth in descent from Ezra. He is wise, so if anyone puts a difficult question to him, he will be able to answer it. He is rich; in case he has to pay honor to Caesar, he will be able to do so. He is tenth in descent from Ezra, so he has ancestral merit and Rabban Gamaliel cannot harm him.

b. Berakhot 27b

Rabbi Eleazar ben Azariah, who, the text reports, is only eighteen years old (sixteen in the Jerusalem Talmud's version) at the time of his appointment, is chosen to be Gamaliel's successor, but it is interesting to note that Akiva's name is mentioned first and then rejected because he lacks "ancestral merit." The fact that Akiva even appears here as an option suggests that on the basis of a combination of intellectual skill and character, he is the obvious choice to take Rabban Gamaliel's place. But status in the rabbinic world is based on a number of factors; as we see in the description of Eleazar, wealth and family background are two that are not available to Akiva. Akiva represents a new model of rabbinic hero that was just being born—a meritocracy based on the person's innate abilities and demonstrated accomplishments.[5] Of course, the world never works quite along those lines, neither in the past nor today. The two pillars of riches and the status of distinguished ancestry never go out of fashion, but this story helps promote an alternative model, a third way that differs from the other two, and Akiva is the finest example in the early formation of Judaism.

The story as told in the Babylonian Talmud merely states that Akiva is not chosen because he lacks the proper family background and hence is vulnerable to harm in retribution from the well-connected Rabban Gamaliel. But the version recorded in the Jerusalem Talmud adds a moving element:

> They appointed Rabbi Eleazar ben Azariah to head the academy. . . . And Rabbi Akiva was sitting, hurt that he had not been chosen. And he said, "It is not that Eleazar knows more

Torah than I do but that he is descended from greater men than I am. Happy is the person whose ancestors have gained merit for him. Happy is the person who has a 'peg' on which to hang."

And what was Rabbi Eleazar ben Azariah's "peg"? That he was the tenth generation in descent from Ezra.

y. Berakhot 4:1

From a literary point of view this version of the story gives us a remarkable moment of insight into Akiva's inner life. He is not a man without ego, as much as we have seen his modesty in other instances. He knows his worth and abilities. But he is bitterly aware of what fate has handed him: he has neither wealth nor worthy parentage. For modern readers, of course, there is some recompense here. We know that even without becoming the Patriarch, the name of Akiva will later far outstrip even the worthy Eleazar. But in the poetic imagination of the Jerusalem Talmud, Akiva has a bitter pill to swallow.

And as if to put an exclamation point on the question of family merit versus talent, as the story continues, Rabbi Eleazar goes on to open up the doors of the Beit Midrash to the many students whom Gamaliel had left outside:

That day they removed the guard from the gate and gave permission for students to enter. For Rabban Gamaliel had issued a proclamation saying: "No student whose inside is not like his outside may enter the Beit Midrash." On that day many benches were added [to accommodate all the new students].

b. Berakhot 28a

Even though Eleazar himself came from a wealthy and socially significant family, he began a process—to use a somewhat anachronistic word—to democratize the academy. One talmudic source claims that four hundred new benches were added—

another says seven hundred. No matter what the precise number, the Talmud emphasizes a change in the composition of the rabbinic community.

The clause "whose inside is not like his outside" is used elsewhere in the Talmud (b. Yoma "The Day" 72b) to indicate a person who puts on a nice show for others that does not conform to his inner, true self—a morally deceptive person in other words. But here I think it is meant to indicate that the study hall is now open to those without finery, those who lack status. Akiva is already one of those and so is his teacher Rabbi Joshua. Indeed, Akiva's strong personal connection to Joshua may in part emanate from the fact that neither of them has great wealth or family reputation. (In contrast, Rabbi Eliezer ben Hyrcanus, Akiva's sometime teacher, sometime nemesis, comes from a landowning family.)

As our story continues, we see Rabban Gamaliel himself begin to change. He worries that he has been "withholding Torah from Israel" by restricting membership in the Beit Midrash. And, in a sign of true character, Gamaliel continues to participate in the deliberations of the academy even though he has been deposed from its leadership. As he watches what is going on, he comes to realize his errors and seeks out Rabbi Joshua at Joshua's home to apologize:

> When Rabban Gamaliel reached Rabbi Joshua's house, he saw that the walls were black. He said to him: "From the walls of your house it is apparent that you are a smith" [the Jerusalem Talmud version has Joshua making needles for his livelihood —an even lowlier job].
>
> Rabbi Joshua replied: "Alas for the generation of which you are the leader, for you do not know the pain of the scholars, how they have to support themselves and sustain themselves!"
>
> Rabban Gamaliel said to him: "I apologize. Forgive me." Rabbi Joshua paid no attention to him. "Do it," Rabban Ga-

maliel said, "out of respect for my father." Joshua then forgave him.

b. Berakhot 28a

Then word is sent to the rabbis by a messenger that Rabban Gamaliel and Rabbi Joshua have become reconciled, but Akiva is suspicious of this news. He doesn't trust the messenger and believes that this may be a ruse perpetrated by a servant of Rabban Gamaliel's: "Rabbi Akiva said, 'Lock the doors so that the servants of Rabban Gamaliel cannot come in and upset the sages.'" Obviously, emotions are running high—fear and suspicion. Finally Rabbi Joshua himself comes, knocks on the door of the Beit Midrash, and says that indeed he and Gamaliel have been reconciled. The next day Joshua and Akiva go together to Gamaliel to announce his reinstatement to leadership.

These stories about Rabbi Joshua and Rabban Gamaliel are concerned both with bowing to the might of leadership and with, in the case of the dispute about the calendar, the power of the rabbis to be the final arbitrators of God's law. Of all the narratives in the rabbinic canon that focus on these issues, none has been more extensively explored in recent years than "The Oven of Akhnai," a short tale in the Babylonian Talmud that has profoundly fascinated readers in our time. This story has occasioned exploration by historical and literary scholars, feminist scholars, legal theorists, Jewish theologians from a wide variety of perspectives, and writers oriented toward the general reader. Here I draw upon the particularly thoroughgoing and careful analysis done by Jeffrey Rubenstein. Rubenstein sees the story as a whole, within its talmudic context, and in doing so, he emphasizes both its literary elements and its truly tragic dimensions.[6]

My own interest here is with the place of the story within the imagined biography of Rabbi Akiva, and therefore I present a somewhat shortened version of the events. The story begins with a debate among the sages about a question related to a topic of great importance in biblical and rabbinic culture and one that is rather remote to us today: the matter of ritual purity. According to the Bible and rabbinic law, people and even objects can acquire "impurity," mainly through contact with death or disease. People or objects that have become impure cannot have any contact with the Temple or other holy places, and in order to dispose of this impurity, a set of rituals was laid out, such as we see described in the books of Leviticus and Deuteronomy in the Bible and expanded upon by the rabbis.

But some objects are constructed in such a way that they cannot be purified. There is some similarity here to the rules of keeping kosher followed by observant Jews today: some dishes or pots and pans can become "unkosher" by contact with a nonkosher product or by mixing milk and meat products in the same implement. Depending on the materials used and the way the object has been made, it might be possible to make it kosher again through boiling it or subjecting it to high temperatures, for example; but other objects cannot be made kosher again no matter what.

In the matter of ritual purity, in most cases it is fairly clear in rabbinic literature which objects can be purified and which cannot, but certain items fall into an ambiguous category. The talmudic debate in our story begins with one of those confusing objects—a particular oven, known as the oven of Akhnai. Akhnai is a proper name, but the story never tells us who Akhnai might be. The rabbis may be talking about the way that this unknown Akhnai has constructed his oven. Or perhaps this is a brand name; that is, an "Akhnai oven" is like a "General Electric stove." At any rate what characterizes the Akhnai oven, according to the Mishnah, is that it is cut into sections, with sand placed between each section. For the rabbis this raises a question: according to rabbinic law, if a clay oven becomes ritually impure, such as through contact with a dead creature, it cannot be purified. But is the Akhnai oven truly a clay oven? The segmented nature of its construction complicates the question. The Mishnah tells us that Rabbi Eliezer ben Hyrcanus ruled that the oven can be purified and the sages ruled that it cannot. With that background the Talmud expands upon the Mishnah's terse statement of the debate and fills in the story with considerable detail:

> On that day Rabbi Eliezer responded with all the responses in the world, but they [the rabbis] did not accept them from him.
>
> Eliezer said to them: "If the law is as I say, let the carob tree prove it." The carob tree uprooted itself from its place and moved one hundred cubits—and some say four hundred cubits.[7] They said to him: "We don't bring proof from a carob tree."
>
> Eliezer said to them, "If the law is as I say, let the stream of water prove it." The water flowed backwards. They said to him: "We don't bring proof from water."
>
> Eliezer said to them: "If the law is as I say, let the walls of the Beit Midrash prove it." The walls of the Beit Midrash inclined to fall. Rabbi Joshua rebuked the walls, saying, "When sages defeat each other in law, what business is it of yours?"
>
> It was taught: They did not fall because of the honor of Rabbi Joshua and they did not stand because of the honor of Rabbi Eliezer and they are still inclining and standing.
>
> Rabbi Eliezer said to them, "If the law is as I say, let it be proved from heaven." A heavenly voice went forth and said: "What is it for you with Rabbi Eliezer since the law is according to him in every place?"
>
> Rabbi Joshua stood on his feet and quoted scripture, "It is not in heaven" (Deuteronomy 30:12).
>
> What did he mean?
>
> Rabbi Jeremiah said, "The Torah was already given on Mount Sinai, so we do not listen to a heavenly voice. It is

written in the Torah, 'After the majority one must incline'"
(Exodus 23:2).

[Later] Rabbi Nathan came upon Elijah and asked him,
"What was the Holy One doing at that time?" Elijah said to
him, "He laughed and smiled and said 'My sons have defeated me, My sons have defeated me.'"

b. Bava Metzia "The Middle Gate" 59b[8]

Writers interested in the theological or legal aspects of the
story usually end the retelling here. It makes a good deal of
sense: we have seen a debate about the nature of law and authority, and, as Rubenstein puts it: "In dramatic fashion the rabbis
assert not only that the majority has authority over the minority but that the sages have authority over God! The sages reject
both miracles supporting the minority opinion of R. Eliezer
and a heavenly voice stating explicitly that the law follows his
opinion with the famous words, 'It is not in Heaven.' . . . That
is, the Torah is no longer in God's control in Heaven but has
been entrusted to the rabbis on earth to interpret and adminis-
ter."[9] The story ends with a nice coda: one of the sages bumps
into the mysterious Elijah the prophet, still visiting the mundane world after his miraculous ascension to heaven in the Bible.
And Elijah informs him that God was laughing, pleased that the
rabbis had defeated him!

But the story as told in the Talmud does not end at this
point. It takes a surprising and disturbing turn:

At that time they brought all the objects that Rabbi Eliezer
had ruled were pure and burned them and voted and banned
him.

They said, "Who will go and inform him?"

Rabbi Akiva said to them: "I will go lest a person who is
not right for this task informs him and in doing so destroys
the entire world." What did he do? He dressed in black and
wrapped himself in black and took off his shoes and sat be-

fore him at a distance of four cubits and his eyes streamed with tears.

Rabbi Eliezer said to him, "Akiva, why is this day different from other days?"

Akiva said to him: "It seems to me that your colleagues are keeping separate from you." Eliezer's eyes too streamed with tears, and he took off his shoes and sat on the ground.

b. Bava Metzia 59b

Eliezer has been excommunicated—the other sages will now be "keeping separate" from him. For Eliezer, indeed for any of the rabbis, what could be a worse punishment? The life of the rabbis, as we see it described in the Talmud and other classical texts, is a world of community, of conversation and the shared enterprise of Torah study. Elsewhere the Talmud discusses these bans and likens them to restrictions on lepers and on those in mourning.[10] Indeed, that is what Eliezer will now become—as if struck with a dread disease, he will be a man outside the community and one who is in constant mourning.

The theme of death and mourning is obvious here in Akiva's behavior—he comes dressed in black and his eyes are filled with tears. Sitting at a distance from Eliezer he symbolizes the separation that Eliezer will now experience from the world of which he has been part.

As Rubenstein points out, the act of burning all the items that Rabbi Eliezer has declared to be pure is shocking: "What provoked them to adopt such harsh measures is not completely clear. . . . The sages apparently wish to take revenge at his having defied them in the first place or attempt to teach him a lesson. In any case the punishment far outstrips the crime, a nonconformist opinion concerning an unusual type of oven."[11] But when the time comes to inform Eliezer of his excommunication, they are in a quandary. Who will take him the bad news? Interestingly, given Akiva's difficult history with Eliezer, it is

Akiva who volunteers for the job. His explanation—"I will go lest a person who is not right for this task informs him and in doing so destroys the entire world"—indicates two things. First, Akiva (and the other sages, one assumes) is worried about the consequences of what they have done. What will ensue from Eliezer's wrath? Indeed, in the continuation of the story after the section quoted above, terrible things do happen: "The world was smitten in one-third of the wheat, one-third of the olives, and one-half of the barley. . . . The destruction was so great on that day that every place where Rabbi Eliezer cast his eyes immediately was burned." Later on, at the conclusion of this tragic tale, the anger of Eliezer leads directly to the death of Rabban Gamaliel, who is struck down by God in response to Eliezer's prayers.

But it is clear that Akiva is worried about something else as well—how to tell such bad news while mitigating the pain that Eliezer will surely feel. In my translation "a person who is not right for this task," I have tried to capture the twofold sense of the Hebrew word (*hagun*) used in the text. On the one hand it implies someone who is "worthy," a person of the proper standing. But it also connotes a person who would know how to conduct himself in the best way possible. Yes, Akiva recognizes his own status among the rabbis; he is not without ego. Yet at the same time, despite their stormy history, he remains Rabbi Eliezer's student and wishes to show compassion to his teacher at this terrible hour. More than that, Akiva trusts his own humane qualities, his empathy and, as we saw in chapter 4, his ability to give rebuke.

We see that sensitivity in the very way that Akiva approaches Eliezer here. Akiva is dressed in mourning clothes and removes his shoes, as is the practice of a mourner. As Rubenstein points out, Akiva "responds equivocally ('it seems to me') and tactfully, not mentioning the ban but employing the neutral and somewhat ambiguous terminology of 'separation.'"[12] And Akiva cannot contain his tears, even for Eliezer, who has at times treated him badly.

In both the story about Rabbi Joshua's conflict with Rabban Gamaliel and the story of Rabbi Eliezer's banishment, we see Akiva in the role of comforter. In both cases Akiva goes out of his way to try to assuage the pain that others are feeling. We see this aspect of Akiva's character in other places as well, often offering comfort through inventive interpretations of biblical verses.[13] But with Eliezer ben Hyrcanus, no textual insight can offer comfort, for no comfort can be had. With Eliezer, Akiva's empathy leads him only to shared mourning and tears.

The story of the oven of Akhnai highlights Akiva's empathy, and that dimension is appropriate to a reading that fits the larger context of the tale. While it is tempting to focus, as many writers have, on the nature of the legal process and the role of human authority that we see in the middle section of the story, the deeply emotional second part of the story may truly be its main theme. As Rubenstein shows, the story is presented in the Talmud in the midst of an extended discussion not about the nature of law, but rather about the ethical sin of "wronging through words." The oven of Akhnai story seems to be intended as a detailed examination of this moral offense.

Rubenstein brings his discussion to a close with the sudden death of Rabban Gamaliel—struck down, it appears, by Eliezer's prayer. But in fact we can see a final conclusion to the story elsewhere, bringing with it an end to the long and difficult drama of Akiva's relationship to his teacher, a sequence of stories that is almost a novella in its length and complexity.

Eliezer has been "banned"; according to the Talmud's restrictions he is not permitted to even say "shalom" to his friends. He is a pariah in the community. He can take on only menial labor, and, most importantly for Rabbi Eliezer, he cannot teach Torah. He can only study by himself.[14]

The finale of the story is told in the Babylonian Talmud

tractate Sanhedrin ("Law Court" 68a). Eliezer is lying on his deathbed, and Akiva and the other sages come to see him. We have no inkling of why they have chosen this moment to visit after what appears to be a long time following his excommunication. Perhaps word has come to them that he is approaching the end of his life. Perhaps they feel guilty about what they have done.

He looks at them and asks them why they have finally come. "To learn Torah," they reply. And quite reasonably he asks them, "Why have you waited until now?" Their answer is both realistic and shocking in its clarity: "We didn't have time." His comment back to them shows the anger and the hurt that he has been feeling since they rejected him. He utters a bitter response, indeed a curse. As if speaking to himself, he remarks, "I would be surprised if these die a natural death." At that moment Akiva turns to him and asks, "And what about my death?" Eliezer replies, "Your death will be more difficult than theirs." In fact, he is telling the truth about Akiva's future, and his comment recalls the same prediction about Akiva's end that he uttered back when Akiva was his student, as we discussed in the last chapter.

Why this special antagonism toward Akiva? After all, it was Akiva who tried so hard to tell him the news about the ban with kindness and sympathy. But perhaps it has become impossible for Eliezer to disassociate Akiva from the events that led to his unhappy fate; perhaps Akiva's status among the other sages has only magnified him in Eliezer's eyes as the representative or symbol of the community of rabbis that has rejected him.

Or perhaps a much older story is at play here, going back to the very beginning of the relationship between these two rabbis. On his deathbed Eliezer recalls the student who has overturned the mountain that Eliezer helped create, the upstart who has outshone him. Eliezer recalls old jealousies and embarrassments, as the young student overtook the teacher and became the hero among his colleagues—all this is too much for Eliezer to bear and he lashes out with a prophecy that will eventually come to pass. Akiva's death will be particularly cruel.

When the Sabbath concludes, Akiva goes out to meet the funeral procession as it moves from Caesarea to Lod where Eliezer will be buried. Despite all the years of conflict and despite the angry last words that Eliezer has spoken to him, Akiva is distraught. In grief, the Talmud reports, "he beat his flesh until the blood flowed down upon the earth" and he quotes the words of shocked despair spoken by the prophet Elisha as his master, Elijah, is carried up to heaven, "My father, my father, the chariot of Israel and its horsemen!" (2 Kings 2:12). And with that scene ends the long and complex story of their relationship.

6

—◆◆◆—

In the Orchard

OF ALL THE STORIES about Akiva, it is probably fair to say that none has occasioned as much discussion and as much debate as this one:

> Four entered the orchard. One looked and died. One looked and was stricken. One looked and cut down the shoots. One went up in peace and came down in peace. Ben Azzai looked and died. . . . Ben Zoma looked and was stricken. . . . Aher looked and cut down the shoots. . . . Rabbi Akiva went up in peace and came down in peace. . . .
>
> A parable was offered: To what might this matter be compared? It is like a king's orchard with an upper chamber built above it. What should a person do? Look, but let him not feast his eyes upon it.
>
> t. Hagigah "Festival Offering" 2:3–5[1]

The story appears in four different versions within the classic literature of rabbinic Judaism: in the Tosefta (quoted above), in the Jerusalem Talmud, in the Babylonian Talmud, and in the midrashic commentary Song of Songs Rabbah. Despite some significant differences the main elements remain the same across the four texts.[2] Scholars have carefully compared the accounts, exploring their similarities and differences, parsing their language and details of plot, discussing the dating and origins of the texts, and, most of all, using these explorations to ponder how we might understand this perplexing tale.

The story is often called "The Pardes Story" after the Hebrew word for orchard, *pardes* (sometimes translated as "garden"), that is its setting. *Pardes* is a loanword, probably from Persian (it is still used in modern Hebrew), and significantly, it is related to the Greek word from which we derive "paradise" in English. Such a word usage virtually calls out for metaphoric interpretation! But what exactly is the story trying to tell us? Is it meant to be read as a historical account of an event? Is it a parable? A piece of literary fiction?

For us, concerned as we are with an exploration of an imagined life of Akiva, looking at the tale may give us another kind of perspective on the way that the texts of the tradition understand the nature of this man. But parsing its meaning and its significance in Akiva's biography is no small task. Academic scholars have tended to view the Tosefta version of the story as the earliest of the various retellings in the tradition.[3] As time passed, this argument asserts, more details were added and the story became more complicated and elaborate. But, as is the case with all the tales within the rabbinic canon, the history of transmission—essentially hidden from our eyes—takes a long and mysterious path. And even if the "purest" (that is, the earliest) version of the story is the one found in the Tosefta, as heirs to the *entire* literary tradition of Judaism now more than fifteen hundred years later, we inherit *all* the tellings in all their permutations.

Our task, at any rate, differs from that of the historical

scholar; our question is, "Who is the Akiva who emerges from the various traditions of the pardes story?" That is the issue with which a biography of Akiva must grapple.

More than seventy years ago Gershom Scholem, the greatest scholar of Jewish mysticism in the twentieth century, delivered an influential lecture that touched upon the pardes story in describing the origins of the mystical element in Judaism.[4] Within the early Jewish tradition there is a significant esoteric literature—dating more or less to the same time as the more familiar talmudic materials—known by scholars as the Hekhalot (the word in Hebrew for palaces) texts or Merkavah (the word in Hebrew for chariot) mysticism. Though some mystical *elements* are found in parts of the Bible and in some of the early prerabbinic literature such as that around the Qumran community, Merkavah mysticism is generally considered the first developed expression of a fully realized Jewish mystical perspective. The question of the relationship between this mystical literature and the better known works of rabbinic literature such as the Babylonian Talmud is one that has been debated in scholarly circles for decades.[5] But it is clear that even in some of the more "conventional" talmudic texts we can see what the scholar Peter Schäfer has called "the infiltration into the Rabbinic literature . . . of material that is part and parcel of Merkavah mysticism."[6]

In Scholem's lecture and in his subsequent writing he suggested that the pardes story represents a report of an actual mystical experience and the consequences of that experience for the four individuals who appear in the tale. As time passed Scholem's interpretation was disputed by scholars who held different views about the pardes story—perhaps the story should be read as a parable; perhaps it is an allegory about four different types of Torah scholars and not about mysticism at all—while still others came to the defense of Scholem's position or adapted it slightly. Whether or not the story is a mystical "testimony," Scholem's comment from years ago still seems relevant: at the very least the pardes narrative is warning about the potential *dangers* of encountering the mystical realm, and to my mind it is hard to dissociate the story from some kind of actual experience.[7]

Mysticism in its Jewish expression, to simplify a very complex subject, can be seen to encompass two different domains: one is mystical *experience;* the other is contemplative or interpretive *speculation.*[8] The former involves the powerful, perhaps even overwhelming sense that one has stepped outside one's normal day-to-day life to encounter in some fashion the divine itself. The other is the intellectual exploration of complex and profound texts about the nature of God and of reality itself. These two domains can be related, but they need not be. One can be involved in mystical practices (such as meditation techniques) without being an interpreter of mystical texts, and one can interpret mystical texts and concepts without having had actual ecstatic experiences. Of course both sides mesh together well; mystical experience can lead one to reflect upon the big questions about the meaning of existence and to delve into literature that is relevant to those issues. And certainly a person who is studying these powerful texts may be led to mystical experiences. Indeed, there may be particular meditative or contemplative exercises *learned* through such study that can lead one to have such extraordinary experiences.

These mystical moments are usually described as being "beyond words," almost indescribable. Mystical reports therefore tend to rely on metaphors, parables, and images to communicate what has happened to an individual. Often this is described as a "vision," which may be accompanied by sound or music or physical sensations (heat or cold or the feeling of rushing wind on the body). One of the most common metaphors for mystical experience in a variety of religions is that of "ascent." A person feels that he or she has been elevated into God's dwelling place. A particularly Jewish image, dating back to the Bible (in particular, chapters 1 and 10 in the book of Ezekiel) and especially powerful in early Jewish mystical writings, is that of entering the many rooms of God's palace or seeing the throne in God's palace as mounted on a chariot. The idea of ascending to an esoteric realm connects directly to the pardes tale: Akiva, after all, "*went up* in peace and *came down* in peace."[9]

The pardes story touches upon both the experiential and the interpretive sides of Jewish mysticism, and perhaps that is why it has inspired so much discussion. The occasion for the story in virtually all the rabbinic sources is a discussion about a statement in the Mishnah that places restrictions on specula-tion both about the Merkavah, the mystical chariot-throne of God, and about the origins of creation. The Mishnah states that these types of exploration should be done only in the com-pany of others or are forbidden unless one has attained a level of wisdom that one can clearly demonstrate beforehand. Hence the Mishnah states that a student should not be taught about the Merkavah unless that student is "one who was wise and understood it on his own" (m. Hagigah 2:1). The comment is clearly paradoxical: you can learn about the Merkavah from a teacher only if you've already discovered the knowledge on your own. But perhaps this is simply the Mishnah's way of say-ing that only certain very talented individuals can engage in mystical speculation. The Mishnah goes on to state that think-ing too much about the origins of the universe is a dangerous activity, though it does not clarify why:

> Anyone who looks into four matters, it would be better for him had he not come into the world: what is above and what below; what is before and what after. Whoever has no con-cern for the honor of his creator—it would be better for him had he not come into the world.
>
> m. Hagigah 2:1

In these examples we are warned about the danger but not told what the nature of that danger might be. But from the Mishnah's point of view both matters are to be avoided: engaging in speculation about what the texts call "the work of the chariot" of God (namely, exploring the nature of the divine) and "looking into" matters related to creation and its antecedents.

The Mishnah's prohibitions are the starting point for a series of stories told in the literature that comes after the Mishnah meant quite obviously to elucidate these prohibitions. First a tale is told about two of the earliest sages, Rabban Yohanan ben Zakkai and Rabbi Eleazar ben Arakh. Eleazar wants Yohanan to teach him about the Merkavah, but Yohanan first needs to be persuaded that Eleazar has the right level of already-acquired wisdom to study this restricted subject matter. The story shows how Eleazar is able to prove his competence to Yohanan.

In a particularly beautiful passage, the version of the story in the Babylonian Talmud tells what happens when Eleazar ben Arakh proves himself to Rabban Yohanan:

> When Rabbi Eleazar ben Arakh began his teaching about the work of the chariot, fire came down from heaven and encircled all the trees in the field. They [the trees] all began to burst forth in song. What was the song they uttered? "Praise the Lord from the earth you sea monsters and all ocean depths . . . fruit trees and all cedars . . . Hallelujah" (Psalm 148:7–14). An angel answered from the fire and said: "This! This is the work of the chariot!"
>
> Rabban Yohanan ben Zakkai stood up and kissed Rabbi Eleazar on his head saying, "Blessed be the Lord, God of Israel who has given a descendent to our father Abraham, Eleazar ben Arakh, who knows how to understand, uncover, and explain the work of the divine chariot!"
>
> b. Hagigah 14b

The Talmud is describing a full-blown mystical experience brought about through the explication of the chariot given by Rabbi Eleazar ben Arakh. Here the connection between mystical understanding and mystical experience, interpretation, and practice is made very clear. It is the *knowledge* that Eleazar has to "understand, uncover, and explain" that has brought down fire from heaven, caused nature to turn to song, and called forth an angelic confirmation of his powers.

The story of Rabbi Eleazar ben Arakh and Rabban Yohanan ben Zakkai is followed by a description of the chain of tradition handing down this secret wisdom within a small set of teachers and students. We learn that Yohanan ben Zakkai taught the mysteries of the "chariot" to Rabbi Joshua, and Rabbi Joshua taught this esoteric knowledge to Rabbi Akiva. Given what we've seen about Joshua and Akiva, it is not surprising both that Akiva had the necessary prerequisite qualities to learn these secrets from his teacher and that Joshua would be willing to teach his prize student what he knew.

It is immediately following the description of the chain of mystical tradition that we find the famous story of the four who entered the orchard. Despite some interesting differences in the telling of the story, the essential structure in the various textual traditions consists of four elements in this order: a statement of the Mishnah's prohibitions on mystical practice and speculation, followed by the story of Rabban Yohanan and Rabbi Eleazar ben Arakh, followed by the description of the chain of teachers and students that culminates in Rabbi Akiva, and followed finally by the pardes story and its aftermath.

It seems clear that the study of the chariot is restricted to small numbers of students precisely because it may *lead* to the kind of mystical experience that we have seen in the example of Eleazar ben Arakh. The pardes story takes this one step farther, showing that such experiences may be dangerous: those who engage in mystical experiences must be wary because they might meet a terrible fate—after all, only Akiva survived intact. The other issue, raised in the Mishnah—the prohibition about speculation on what came before creation and its attendant mysteries—is not part of the equation at this point, though it will emerge a bit later.

Those who are able to "ascend" into the realm of the divine, the rabbinic sources show us, are tapping into a source of energy that carries with it great benefits but also supreme dangers. To do what the tradition calls the "work" of the Merkavah, one is approaching the inner core of reality itself. It is, as mystical texts will sometimes say, like staring at the sun—great light, but also the danger of being blinded. To use a metaphor more familiar to us: the way these texts present coming near to the chariot is analogous to the way we might think about a nuclear reactor—it offers the potential for benefit and for harm, warmth and destruction. The pardes story explores the two-edged sword of the mystical encounter.

Four enter the orchard, but only Akiva escapes unharmed. Ben Azzai is so overwhelmed (or as some rabbinic interpreters understand it, he is so beloved by God) that he dies. Ben Zoma "looked and was stricken." As the text continues in the Tosefta a few pages later it is clear that this means that Ben Zoma went mad from the experience.

The fourth member of the group that entered the orchard is called Aher. This is a pejorative nickname—"Aher" means "the other"—for Elisha ben Abuya. In the story we are told that Aher "cut down the shoots," a strange metaphor meant to indicate that he has become a heretic. This Elisha is one of the most fascinating and perplexing characters in rabbinic literature. He has come to symbolize the ultimate figure of one who has left the fold, but as scholars have noted, when Elisha appears in the earliest strata of rabbinic writings, he is treated as a quotable scholar without any taint of his later negative reputation.[10]

Considerable literature is devoted to discussing the history of Elisha—how he became a sinner, what the nature of his sin was, and how he got the nickname Aher. But the complicated interweaving of traditions and the inconsistency in the portrayal of Elisha from the earliest texts to the later versions make it nearly impossible to disentangle a straightforward narrative from these various pieces, never mind finding whatever core of a "historical" Elisha may be embedded here.

Linking the stories of Elisha to the pardes story raises a related set of issues: Was Elisha already an apostate by the time he joined the others in the journey to the orchard? And if so, what was he doing with the other three saintly men? He is, of course, already called Aher in the pardes story, but perhaps that is only because the tale is told retrospectively when Aher's sinfulness is already known. From a literary point of view there is a good deal to be said for the interpretation offered by the version of the story in the Babylonian Talmud: namely, it is the experience that Elisha has in the orchard that leads to his apostasy.[11] Of course, we do not know what precisely occurred that led him in that direction, but that is not surprising. Neither do we know what caused Ben Azzai to die and Ben Zoma to go mad. Nonetheless, knowing the terrible consequences for three of the participants leads us to the conclusion that something extraordinarily powerful happened that day.

And thus we are led back to the original question that has been debated about this narrative for so long: Is the pardes story a report of an experience? Scholem used the more elaborate version in the Babylonian Talmud for his discussion of the story. That version adds an interesting element that makes the event seem quite palpable in its recounting of detail. Right after we read that four entered the orchard, the text quotes Rabbi Akiva speaking to the other three: "When you draw near the stones of pure marble, do not say 'Water! Water!' for it is written 'The speaker of lies shall not be established in my sight' (Psalm 101:7)" (b. Hagigah 14b). In other words, as they are about to "enter" the orchard of a mystical vision, Akiva warns the others about the tricks that their eyes and mind may play on them. And the orchard he describes does not resemble a place of trees and flowers, but rather the story references the way that the rooms of God's palace are described in the early mystical literature. Be careful, he tells them, do not be fooled into thinking that you are looking at water when in reality you are seeing the pure marble in God's own palace. It seems obvious that the peculiar detail of the stones that look like water is part of a test. As Schäfer puts it, Akiva is telling them, "If you cannot refrain from exclaiming 'water, water'—presumably because you are so frightened by the view of the radiant stones—you are a 'liar,' that is, you do not belong where you are and you will be forbidden from seeing God."[12]

The notion that the orchard was the heavenly palace of God and was visited by these four eminent figures is one that has held a good deal of weight within later Jewish tradition. For example, the eleventh-century sage Hai Gaon understood the pardes story as "an ecstatic celestial journey."[13] Rashi (eleventh-century France), the most influential commentator on the Talmud, states quite baldly that the four who entered the orchard "went up to the heavens through use of the divine name."[14] Indeed, for the later tradition the only debate seems to have been about whether the four *actually* went up to the divine palace or only *thought* they had ascended.[15]

Here, we clearly can see the pardes story as yet another "hero tale" about Rabbi Akiva, though in this story we see him as a different kind of hero from what we've seen in the earlier stories. Akiva in this tale is a spiritual master, a person capable of attaining an insight into God and God's hidden realm that other worthy figures were unable to attain. But why did Akiva succeed while the other three who entered the orchard suffered such terrible fates? How did he differ from the rest of them?

The scholar C. R. A. Morray-Jones may have been the first to highlight a detail from the story that is so obvious it is easy to overlook: of the four who entered the orchard, only Akiva is called by the title "rabbi." When the Mishnah states that exploration of the Merkavah should be done only by "one who was wise and understood it on his own," the word for "wise" used there is *hakham*, the same word translated as "sage" (equivalent to "rabbi") when used as a noun. Morray-Jones suggests that the text is saying that only a rabbi should be exploring these mysteries, and of the four who entered the orchard, wise as they all may have been, only Akiva was a rabbi.[16]

But "ordination" as a rabbi is a murky area in the early stages of Judaism, as I've already mentioned. More important in gaining access to the mystical side of the tradition, it seems to me, was having a teacher who properly initiated the student into the esoteric domain of the "work of the chariot." And of course we know from these texts that Akiva *did* have a teacher in these matters, Rabbi Joshua, the same teacher who, as we've seen, was with him from the beginning of his studies, the teacher who recognized his brilliance (in a way that Eliezer ben Hyrcanus did not), and the teacher who had learned the mystical secrets directly from Rabban Yohanan ben Zakkai himself.

But having the status of rabbi and having a teacher who instructed him may not be the only reason for Akiva's success. In a subtle reading, the scholar Alon Goshen-Gottstein points out another difference between Akiva and the other three who entered the orchard.[17] Ben Azzai, Ben Zoma, and Aher all "looked" at the garden—but the word "look" does not appear when Akiva is described. The text simply says he "went up in peace and came down in peace." Goshen-Gottstein sees the parable that immediately follows in our text as explaining the significance of the difference around the word "look":

> To what might this matter be compared? It is like a king's
> orchard with an upper chamber built above it. What should
> a person do? Look, but let him not feast his eyes upon it.

t. Hagigah 2:5

Goshen-Gottstein suggests that this parable, by its place on the page, is intended to explicate the meaning of the "four who entered" story. There is an orchard certainly, but there is also another structure present, "an upper chamber" that sits above the orchard. In other parables in rabbinic literature that use this phraseology, Goshen-Gottstein points out, the "upper chamber" is often the dwelling place of the king. In metaphoric language, in other words, the parable may be alluding to a heavenly palace "above" wherein God (the king) resides. The problem with the three scholars who failed, according to this reading, is that they were distracted by the orchard's beauty; only Akiva aimed at going "above" the orchard to the king's palace.[18]

Most readings of the pardes story focus on the experience of what happened to the four within the orchard itself. This interpretation adds a different possible dimension to how we might understand the events. But even if Goshen-Gottstein has it right, what we really learn from this interpretation is what went wrong for Akiva's comrades. Whether we view the orchard as a distraction, with the upper chamber being the real goal (as Goshen-Gottstein would have it), or whether the real story is about the orchard itself (as most of the classic Jewish commentators saw it), there is no doubt about the success of Akiva in attaining some special insight into the divine. And we learn an additional element of Akiva's success a few pages later in the Babylonian Talmud's telling of these events:

> Rabbi Akiva went up in peace and came down in peace; and
> of him scripture says: "Draw me after you, let us run! The
> king has brought me into his chambers" (Song of Songs 1:4).

And even Rabbi Akiva the ministering angels sought to push away; but the Holy One, blessed be He, said to them: "Leave this elder alone—for he is worthy to make use of my glory."

b. Hagigah 15b

The phrase "to make use of my glory" is confusing to be sure. The great contemporary scholar of Jewish mysticism, Moshe Idel, explains this as meaning that God announces that Akiva "was worthy of the magical *use* of the divine glory."[19] Idel contrasts this with a text from the mystical Hekhalot literature that has Akiva telling in the first person how the angels wished to "destroy" him and how God prevented the angels from doing so, saying, "Leave this elder alone—for he is worthy to *look at* my glory."[20] But no matter which version we consider, the praise for Akiva in these sources is yet another extraordinary testament to his status within the canon of rabbinic Judaism. "The king has brought me into his chambers," that is, God himself has invited Akiva into the inner reaches of the divine mystery.

The midrashic commentary on the Song of Songs also explores the question of why Akiva survived the visit to the orchard intact while the others did not. Like the Hekhalot texts, it has the charming element of Akiva speaking in his own first-person voice about the answer:

It is not because I am greater than my colleagues but because of the teaching in the Mishnah, "Your deeds will bring you near and your deeds will keep you far." The Talmud concludes, "Of him it is said, 'The king has brought me into his chambers'" (Song of Songs 1:4).

Song of Songs Rabbah 1:27

What does it mean for Akiva to say that he is not "greater" than his colleagues when in fact the latter part of the quotation seems to indicate that he *is* greater—that is, his "deeds" (the term usually refers to fulfilling God's commandments) are what brought him near to God?

The most reasonable explanation is probably found in the text from the Mishnah that Akiva quotes. There the text is describing a deathbed scene between two rabbinic figures, a father and son. As the father is dying, the son asks him to seek out the holy individuals who have passed on to their eternal reward and request that they put in a good word for the son in the heavenly realm. The father refuses. "Have I done something to displease you?" asks the son. No, replies the father, and then says the words Akiva quotes: "Your deeds will bring you near and your deeds will keep you far" (m. Eduyot "Testimonies" 5:7).

In other words, it is not on the merit of your father's status but on the merit of your own deeds that you will establish your ultimate rewards in the cosmic realm. As we have seen before, the issue of Akiva's lowly origins continues to play a role in his ongoing self-understanding. When he talks about not being "greater" than his fellows, he means that his ancestry is not more distinguished than theirs. But he *has* attained exemplary status through his own meritorious deeds.

In other early mystical texts we can see a similarly high status accorded to Akiva. In the text known as Hekhalot Zutarti, Akiva follows Moses's example and ascends to the divine throne room.[21] That text presents the pardes story, introducing it as a *first-person* telling in Akiva's own voice. As Peter Schäfer puts it: "It becomes immediately clear why our editors are so keen at quoting it here: Rabbi Akiva is their hero, and he was the only one who ascended and descended in peace. . . . Whatever the original purpose of the four rabbis' entrance into the *pardes* might have been, for our editors it is obvious that the rabbis ascended to the Merkavah, that only Akiva survived this adventure unharmed, and he received there a revelation of the divine name."[22]

But Akiva in the eyes of this mystical literature attains

something beyond the remarkable accomplishment of learning the secret and efficacious name of God. Hekhalot Zutarti shows that, as Schäfer puts it, "Akiva goes much farther than any of his predecessors. He is the only one who knows that God looks like us, like human beings." This is knowledge gained, Schäfer continues, "from the experience of his ascent."[23]

Akiva, in other words, becomes the ultimate model of the Jewish mystic—gaining mystical knowledge and power and seeing the face of the divine. And one of the powerful holds that Akiva comes to have for future generations (and particularly for mystics within the Jewish tradition) is the sense that he knew God in the deepest and most intimate way. "Within a generation or two" after Akiva's death, Goshen-Gottstein writes, "different groups seem to be appropriating him as a hero of mystical activity." The general consensus within the early traditions of Judaism "on the mystical dimension of Rabbi Akiva's activities is important and early testimony regarding a probable spiritual activity of Rabbi Akiva. Thus this document not only teaches concerning R. Akiva's spiritual activities, but also communicates how his figure is associated with such activities not long after his own time."[24] And even more than that, long after the Talmudic Age, Akiva becomes the role model for all those down through Jewish history who wish to attain that kind of intimate and direct connection to the divine.

7

The Last Years

RABBINIC LITERATURE is filled with stories about Akiva. There are stories of his travels—in one he survives a shipwreck; in others he travels to distant lands, even to Rome. But these tales—dealing with the years after he first starts learning Torah —do not fit into a coherent and organized narrative of his life. What do we know about his family? The love story that I recounted in chapter 3, for example, does not yield to an ongoing picture of his married life. We did see there that he "made a 'City of Gold' [diadem] for his wife," perhaps to fulfill his early tender desire in the hayloft to give her a "Jerusalem of Gold," but we have no picture of the couple's ongoing relationship during Akiva's years as a teacher and leader.

Similarly we know virtually nothing about his children. Rabbinic literature recounts a few stories about the death of his sons, but these are told only in passing, in the midst of a discussion about other matters.[1] Unfortunately, few details are given about their lives. One son known as Rabbi Joshua is identified in a passage in the Babylonian Talmud (b. Pesahim "Passover" 112a) in which Akiva is giving advice to his son, and in a passage in the Tosefta (t. Ketubot "Marriage Contracts" 4:7) a case is brought concerning the wedding of "Rabbi Joshua the son of Rabbi Akiva." Some traditions assert that Akiva's student Joshua Ben Karha is actually Akiva's son since in one talmudic source Ben Azzai *may* refer to Akiva as "that bald one" and the name "ben Karha" means "son of the bald-headed one."[2] Is R. Joshua the same as one of the sons who died? Did only one of his sons die? We have no evidence about any of this.

We are told that he had a daughter who behaved the same way as her mother—persuading her future husband, reputed to be Ben Azzai, to study Torah before she would marry him. Yet Ben Azzai is one of the few rabbinic figures who is said never to have married.[3] Once again, as we have often seen, it is difficult, if not impossible, to find consistency among the many stories in rabbinic literature.

With all these details about Akiva's "middle years" missing, it is fortunate that we find a good deal of literature about the last years of his life. Akiva's death is usually placed within the context of historical events in the early second century CE. To explore the end of his life we need first turn to the circumstances of that time as historical scholarship has uncovered them.

As I recounted in chapter 1, the disastrous consequences of the Great Revolt—the destruction of the Temple and the death, enslavement, or exile of large numbers of the Jewish population—brought about a traumatic upending of Jewish life and of the Temple-oriented religious practices of Judaism in the years following 70 CE.[4] What was the response of the Jews going to be? Knowing as we do now that 70 CE marked the end of the Temple for the rest of Jewish history, it is not hard to imagine that the Jews of the first and second centuries had the rebuilding of the Temple most on their minds. As Martin Goodman puts it,

"The Temple had been destroyed, so the task of Jews must be to ensure that, as rapidly as possible, it be rebuilt."[5]

Having the hindsight of history, of course, we know a different narrative: with the end of Temple sacrifices, the essence of the Judaism that is familiar to us today—obviously transmuted and changed over the centuries—came into being. Prayer came to be a substitute for the Temple service; although the Torah had certainly been the essential document of Judaism before the destruction, eventually the *study* of Torah moved to the center of Jewish religious consciousness; atonement was to be gained not through animal sacrifices but through acts of kindness and charity or through an individual's personal suffering.[6] Perhaps the most obvious example is the rabbis' invention of the now familiar ritual of the Passover Seder as a home-based practice that takes the place of the Temple-based paschal sacrifice. When the Mishnah describes the core components of the Seder, writes Baruch Bokser in his classic work on the subject, it is outlining a "process which aims at continuity and cannot acknowledge the existence of change, but which at the same time is motivated by a desire to express a new meaning."[7]

To Jews today such new structures are very familiar, but it took centuries for them to evolve. The Mishnah's description of the Seder, for example, is formulated 150 years after the destruction of the Temple, and the Seder evolved considerably over time after the Mishnah's short chapter outlining the rite. In the years following 70 CE, however, what seemed most familiar was that which had been lost: the world of sacrifices and the function of the priests who managed these rituals. These matters went back to the Bible itself. Following the destruction it was only natural that the Jews expected a new Temple would be built and that they would return to the practices they knew best. After all, it had happened after the destruction of the First Temple in 586 BCE with the return from the Babylonian exile, beginning around 538 BCE; some twenty years later a Second

Temple, modest in scope, was constructed. And during Herod's rule, as we have seen, that Second Temple had been expanded and made magnificent.

Thus even in the ashes of Jerusalem's destruction Jews could imagine that "once the site was sufficiently cleared of rubble (a laborious task), the erection of a modest sanctuary and altar would be a simple matter. Plenty of priests survived to officiate, and presumably some still knew what to do."[8] In other places of Roman rule local populations were allowed to rebuild their temples when they had been destroyed, so wouldn't the Jews have expected this to take place in Jerusalem as well?

But it never happened. Not because the Jews stopped wanting it, but because of "the refusal of the Roman state to permit the Jews to behave like all other religious groups within the empire."[9] It seems likely that the Romans were not terribly eager to have a rebuilt Temple as the focal point for more Jewish revolutionary activities. From the Romans' point of view, it was just as well to leave the Temple in ashes as a reminder of the consequences of revolt.

Internal politics of the Roman world also played a significant role here. The elderly Roman emperor Nerva, who governed from 96 to 98 CE, might well have permitted the Temple to be rebuilt. But his was a short-lived reign, and at his death, he was succeeded by Trajan, whose father had been one of the generals who had fought the Jewish rebels during the Great Revolt. Trajan was not about to throw an olive branch to the Jews of Palestine.

With Trajan's death in 117, Hadrian ascended to the Roman Empire's throne. About a decade after he came to power, Hadrian began rebuilding Jerusalem as a city to be called Aelia Capitolina[10] and constructing a temple for Jupiter on the site of the ruined Jewish Temple. This was an act, as the historian Seth Schwartz puts it, tantamount to "dancing on the Jews' collective grave. He cannot have been unaware of the history of the site."[11] Hence it seems fairly clear that Hadrian's actions were intentional: he wanted to stomp out any hope for future Jewish rebellions or even for a modicum of independence from Rome. Building Aelia Capitolina was a solution to the problem going back to the time of the Great Revolt some sixty years before: "Hadrian's solution was to ensure that Jews could never again expect to have a temple on their sacred site in Jerusalem, by founding a miniature Rome on the site of the Jews' holy city."[12]

But such actions did not result in quelling future rebellion. Eventually, Hadrian got a full-scale uprising in Judaea (by and large the war did not spread beyond the boundaries of Judaea into the rest of Eretz Yisrael) that we now call the Bar Kokhba Revolt or Bar Kokhba War (132–135 CE). Historians have suggested several causes for the revolt, the most well-known being Hadrian's ban on circumcision. Here once again the evidence is unclear. That Hadrian forbade circumcision is not disputed; but whether the ban took place *before* the revolt and indeed helped spark the uprising or whether it was put into effect *after* the end of the war as a punishment for the Jews is hard to determine from the historical record.[13]

One of the many obscurities about the years following 130 CE in Judaea is what Hadrian may have had in mind when he initiated the idea for Aelia Capitolina and the Temple of Jupiter. It is the mystery of how, as Peter Schäfer writes, "Hadrian, the Emperor of peace and renewal, stumbled into such a war so devastating that he needed his full military force to crush it."[14] Perhaps today we should not be so surprised: in the aftermath of the wars in Vietnam and Iraq, we know too well the unintended consequences of military plans. Of course there is a veritable *list* of things that remain unclear about the Bar Kokhba Revolt.[15] And, most importantly for our purposes here, we can add that we do not know with certainty what role, if any, Rabbi Akiva played in the episode.

The name of the leader of the revolt has come down to us

as Bar Kokhba, "son of a star."[16] In rabbinic sources he is usually called Bar Kozba or Bar Koziba, literally meaning "son of deception," indicating that the rabbis viewed the revolt as a catastrophe, as indeed it was. By contrast, the association with "star" speaks of a much loftier view of Bar Kokhba, and this view is directly associated with Rabbi Akiva. The Jerusalem Talmud reports:

> Rabbi Shimon bar Yohai taught: "My teacher Akiva, would interpret the verse 'A star [kokhav] rises from Jacob' (Numbers 24:17) to mean Kozba rises from Jacob."
>
> When Rabbi Akiva beheld Bar Kozba, he exclaimed: "This one is King Messiah!"
>
> Rabbi Yohanan ben Torta said to him: "Akiva, grass will grow between your jaws and the son of David [the Messiah] still will not have come!"
>
> y. Ta'anit "Fast Days" 4:8

Akiva plays off the word *kokhav* (star) in the biblical verse and associates it with the similar-sounding name Kozba. Not only that, but Akiva proclaims that Bar Kokhba is the Messiah, the extraordinary redemptive figure, descendant of the Davidic line, who will restore glory to Israel, or in some views, bring about the end of time. But Yohanan ben Torta is not convinced. "This man is not the Messiah," ben Torta tells him. "The Messiah will not be here so quickly. You will long be dead and we will still be waiting for the Messiah to arrive."

The real name of the leader of the revolt—Shimon ben (or bar) Kosibah—was not unearthed until remarkable archeological discoveries made in the Judaean desert in the twentieth century. This work, first begun in the early 1950s, culminated in the discovery of letters from Shimon himself, found in 1960. Coins from the period stamped with Shimon's name proclaim him to be "nasi Yisrael," a term usually translated as the "prince of Israel" (perhaps more accurately, "leader of Israel"), an honorific title dating back to biblical times. Schäfer points out that the term *nasi* is "much less ideologically loaded" than the title "king," a word that Bar Kokhba seems to have intentionally avoided. (I will follow convention and continue to use the name "Bar Kokhba" that longstanding tradition has willed to us.) Indeed, the only reference to Bar Kokhba as king in rabbinic sources is in Akiva's "King Messiah" exclamation.[17]

But what exactly did this leader Bar Kokhba accomplish? In fact there is an enormous amount that we do not know about him or the revolt. How we read the "Bar Kokhba letters" is also a matter of debate and personal preference. One scholar finds him to be a "demanding leader and a stickler for detail who constantly rebuked his subordinates for failing to fulfill their assignments scrupulously."[18] Another observes that "most of the orders in Bar Kokhba's letters are connected with a threat of punishment, and this coarse tone can be attributed just as much to his character as to his increasingly desperate situation towards the end of the revolt."[19] "Stickler for detail" or "coarse"? Much is left to the eye of the beholder. For Akiva, at least in that one source from the Jerusalem Talmud, Bar Kokhba is the very image of the Messiah. While the general record in rabbinic sources tends strongly toward the negative regarding Bar Kokhba, as I have said, these texts "still recorded tales of his heroic feats. Presumably some Jews remembered him as a great man but a failure, or an attractive fraud. The same sources recount his blood-soaked last stand near the Judaean village Beitar."[20]

Bar Kokhba waged a war against the far superior Roman forces for some three years, beginning in the summer of 132 and ending by and large with the destruction of Beitar in the summer of 135. From the Roman side, this was no small military campaign. It "apparently numbered over 50,000 Roman soldiers. The size of Bar Kokhba's force remains entirely conjectural. Although certainly smaller than the Roman forces, given the antagonists' response it must have numbered in the tens of thousands."[21]

Thus the revolt was no fringe enterprise of a small group of fanatics; Bar Kokhba clearly attracted enough popular support to engage the world's greatest army in a lengthy struggle. Akiva's support of Bar Kokhba may have mirrored the popularity that Bar Kokhba seems to have enjoyed among at least a significant part of the population. But ultimately the Bar Kokhba War was a failure, and rabbinic sources portraying Bar Kokhba as a false Messiah certainly reflect the grim facts. As one historian, commenting on the twentieth-century archeological work, sums up the aftermath: "all Judaean villages, without exception, excavated thus far were razed following the Bar Kokhba Revolt. This evidence supports the impression of total regional destruction following the war."[22] It is no wonder that rabbinic texts viewed Bar Kokhba with such disdain. They might reasonably have felt that his zeal brought all this destruction upon them.

To gauge Akiva's possible connection to Bar Kokhba we should consider the desire for Jewish independence that Akiva may have felt. According to the traditional chronology, Akiva lived through the Great Revolt and the destruction of the Temple in 70 CE. If we take this at its face value for a moment (for of course we have no real evidence about the actual dates of Akiva's life), assuming that Akiva was born around the year 50 CE, we can imagine those early experiences leading to one of two polar reactions to the Bar Kokhba Revolt. Akiva might, on the one hand, have been so traumatized by the events of 66–70 CE that he would have wanted to eschew any future uprising at any cost. But on the other hand, those recollections of his youth may have intensified his desire for independence from Rome. The statement attributed to him in which he views Bar Kokhba as the Messiah seems to lean in the latter direction.

We should also consider carefully what Akiva would have meant by the phrase "King Messiah." Within Jewish tradition there are two competing notions of the meaning of the "messianic age"; both go back at least as far as the Second Temple period, and perhaps earlier. Gershom Scholem describes these two tendencies about messianism as being a "restorative" vision on the one hand and a "utopian" vision on the other. The restorative view sees the messianic age as "directed to the return and recreation of a past condition which comes to be felt as ideal"; the utopian impulse aims "at a state of things which has never yet existed." The restorative hopes for the "reinstitution of an ideally conceived Davidic kingdom"; the utopian vision is apocalyptic—nature itself is turned upside down. In the utopian view we do not reenter history and create an ideal society as in the restorative approach; instead, history itself ends: the wicked are punished, the dead are resurrected, Eden returns, the "catastrophic" "Day of the Lord" arrives, in which "previous history ends and on which the world is shaken to its foundations."[23]

Nowadays, when we hear the words "messiah" or "messianic," we are much more likely to think of the almost magical, "beyond history" vision of the term. But for Akiva the notion of "the Messiah" as a military and political leader aiming to restore an idealized Davidic kingdom was probably just as likely to have been in his mind.[24]

Perhaps in addition Akiva would have been impressed by Bar Kokhba's connection to what we might call Jewish "religious" matters—things that may have appealed to Akiva as a rabbi. Bar Kokhba's "religiosity" (and here I am using a modern term that would not have made much sense to Akiva) is also a matter of considerable debate among scholars. Certainly we know from the letters found in the desert that Bar Kokhba cared that his followers observe the Sabbath. In addition we know from the letters that he ordered the delivery of the "four species"—the palm branch (*lulav*), citron (*etrog*), myrtle, and willows—required to fulfill the observance of the harvest festival of Sukkot. He may have been concerned with proper tithing of agricultural produce—that is, setting aside a part of the harvest for priests—though there is some debate about how to interpret those letters. But did this make him a follower of "the rabbis," and is that why he may have been attractive to Akiva? Peter Schäfer convincingly argues that such a question may have it backwards: we should not be "forcibly and anachronistically imposing on Bar Kokhba and his revolt our pre-conceived image of the Rabbis of the first half of the second century CE."[25] Instead, we should recognize that during this period rabbinic Judaism was in its very earliest stages.

Thus it is hard to gauge how Akiva would have viewed Bar Kokhba's religious inclinations, or even whether he knew about them at all. In fact, all of this discussion about Akiva's connection to Bar Kokhba assumes that there *was* a connection between them—that Akiva either saw or actually met Bar Kokhba, that the rabbi supported the revolt or that the tragic end of Akiva's life was related to his support of the war. But nothing in the formal *historical* record confirms these assumptions.

And so we are left to explore the legends surrounding his association with Bar Kokhba and the fate that overtook Akiva in his final days. One story about Akiva often viewed as connected to the Bar Kokhba Revolt tells the following tragic tale:

> Rabbi Akiva had twelve thousand pairs of students . . . and they all died at the same period of time because they did not treat each other with respect. The world remained desolate until R. Akiva came to our Masters in the South and taught the Torah to them. These were R. Meir, R. Yehudah, R. Yose, R. Shimon, and R. Eleazar b. Shammua; and it was they who raised up the Torah at that time. A Tanna taught: All [of the twelve thousand pairs] died between Passover and Shavuot.

R. Hama b. Abba . . . said: "All of them died a terrible death. What was it?" R. Nahman said, "Diphtheria."[26]

b. Yevamot "Levirate Marriage" 62b

When in the imagined life of Akiva is this story supposed to have taken place, and what is the point that the story is making? This tale is often associated with the final years of Akiva's life; indeed, the death of the disciples has often been viewed as an encoded description of the possible connection between the death of the students and the Bar Kokhba War. Was this an indirect way, some have argued, of telling us that Akiva's students fought in the war and died in battle?

In fact, there is a good deal of internal evidence in the story itself—and in other literary texts in rabbinic literature that touch upon the same events—to argue *against* such an interpretation. To make sense of this tale let us first consider its structure. It has four parts: first we read of the deaths of the disciples and the reason for their deaths; second we see the "desolate" state of the world following these events and Akiva's mission to cultivate a group of five students who would bring Torah into the world again; third, an unnamed rabbi (a Tanna, that is, an unnamed sage from the early period of rabbinic Judaism) tells us when precisely the students died; and fourth, a question is raised about the specific cause of death, and R. Nahman answers it.

The tale, in its details and divorced from any historical speculation, seems to have little to do with the Bar Kokhba Revolt. Aside from the deaths of such a large—and certainly exaggerated—number of people as might occur during war, there is no other evidence for drawing any connection with Bar Kokhba. In fact it makes more sense to place the story much earlier in Akiva's life, as I will show.

If the story is not about the Bar Kokhba War, what does it mean? Before we explore that question, I should mention one point that may explain why this story of the deaths of Akiva's students may be familiar to some readers. In the third part of the story, the unnamed Tanna tells us that the twenty-four thousand students died between the festivals of Passover and Shavuot. But given the way that the story is constructed, this detail appears to be an addition, unrelated to the core of the tale; indeed, an earlier text upon which this story is built—a midrash from Genesis Rabbah—lacks this piece of information. Nonetheless, the story of the deaths of Akiva's students came to have an important association in Jewish religious life. The period of time between Passover and Shavuot is known as the "Counting of the Omer" in Jewish tradition. ("Omer" refers to a measure of grain offered as a sacrifice.) Each day during this seven-week period, Jews are enjoined to count down the days from the first holiday (Passover) to the next (Shavuot) by reciting a blessing and a liturgical formula for announcing the day in the count (as in, "Today is day five of the Omer," etc.).

Why the counting? The Torah does not give an explanation, but one that seems reasonable is that Passover commemorates the Israelites being freed from Egyptian bondage; Shavuot is the holiday that marks the giving of the Torah at Mount Sinai (Exodus 19–20). In the mythic history of the Jewish people, in other words, that period between the two festivals is a time of liberation without the safety and control of the Torah's laws. Hence it is a time of anticipation, but also anxiety. Jewish tradition, in the spirit of this liminal perhaps even dangerous time period, forbids marriages and other celebrations to take place during those seven weeks of the Omer count.

But a different explanation, connected to Akiva, came to be associated with this ban on frivolity as well: dating from around the ninth century CE, one of the leaders of the Babylonian Jewish community, Rav Natronai Gaon, attributed the custom of refraining from joy to memorializing the deaths of Akiva's twenty-four thousand students; and ever since, this story and the customs of the "Omer" period have been linked in Jewish consciousness.

How the narrative of the deaths of the disciples evolved in rabbinic literature is a complex process, and it has been carefully analyzed by the scholar Aaron Amit.[27] Amit shows how the familiar story from the Babylonian Talmud is based on an earlier version of the same events found in the midrashic text Genesis Rabbah (a text rooted in Jewish traditions of Palestine rather than those of Babylonia):

> Rabbi Akiva had twelve thousand pairs of disciples, and all of them died at the same period of time. Why? Because their eyes were narrow with one another. Eventually Rabbi Akiva raised seven disciples: R. Meir, R. Yehudah, R. Yose, R. Shimon, R. Eleazar b. Shammua, R. Yohanan the Cobbler, and R. Eliezer b. Jacob. . . . Rabbi Akiva said: My first sons died only because their eyes were narrow with each other in Torah. See to it that you do not do as they did. They arose and filled all the land of Israel with Torah.
>
> Genesis Rabbah 61:3

Amit demonstrates how the talmudic passage previously cited is a reshaping of this earlier midrashic text in a variety of ways. We can see immediately certain additions in the Talmud's version: for example, the Genesis Rabbah text does not specify the time to the Omer period, nor does it include a medical reason for the deaths, as in the Talmud's version. Amit notes that neither text refers to Bar Kokhba; indeed, in both versions of the tale we see that the story is presented (in one version by Akiva himself) to settle an interpretative debate that immediately precedes the passages I have quoted. In that debate the rabbis are trying to understand the meaning of a biblical verse from Ecclesiastes: "Sow your seed in the morning, and do not hold back your hand in the evening, since you do not know which is going to succeed, the one or the other, or if both are equally good" (11:6). For Akiva the verse is a lesson tinged with sadness. If you have made disciples in your youth, he says, be sure to continue doing so in your old age, for who is to know what will happen to them in the long run? Immediately following this is the tale of Akiva's unfortunate twenty-four thousand disciples as an example to prove his case.

The number of students—twenty-four thousand—may have a familiar ring, as we encountered it back in chapter 3 in the story of Akiva and his wife and the disciples he raised while he was away for twenty-four years. It cannot be an accident that the number in our passages from the Babylonian Talmud and Genesis Rabbah is "twelve thousand pairs" of students. It is in the *early* stage of Akiva's career that he amassed his ill-fated twenty-four thousand students, not at the time of the Bar Kokhba Revolt. The connection of the students' deaths to any role Akiva might have had in the revolt once again makes little sense. The disciples of his later years are the five (or seven) specifically named in our passages.

But the story has a deeper meaning beyond its connection to the details of Akiva's life. The plague that kills the students is only the immediate cause of death; the real reason behind the cause is that their deaths are a divine punishment for some egregious sin. The early Genesis Rabbah version explains the sin as "their eyes were narrow with one another." Amit shows that this is a rabbinic euphemism for stinginess and suggests that "stinginess is not a quality that usually describes scholars."[28]

But I am not so convinced: there is a kind of stinginess that one may find around scholars—perhaps the text is saying that the students lacked *intellectual generosity* with one another, that they failed to share their insights and were stingy in that sense. At any rate, years after the time of the Genesis Rabbah text, the Babylonian Talmud "changed the Palestinian tradition and claimed that the disciples showed disrespect for one another, a quality appropriate in this context."[29]

Thus the story before us is another example of what Jeffrey Rubenstein calls a "didactic tale"—a story meant to convey a lesson.[30] If we take this tale not as a piece of supposed historical reportage but as a moral parable, we can see it as warning about the heavy consequences of a lack of generosity or a lack of respect among scholars. Of course this "punishment" is shocking to modern ears—twenty-four thousand deaths to teach that lesson!—but it makes more sense not to take the narrative literally. The more profound reading is that the "world" suffered the consequences—it was left "desolate" until Rabbi Akiva was able to reconstitute his disciples and build upon this foundation. The Genesis Rabbah version provides a beautiful detail missing from the Talmud's telling, that is, Akiva's warning to his students—a warning that we must assume he meant for all the generations of scholars that came after him: "See to it that you do not do as they did." In other words, he is telling them, the way you treat your colleagues in this work has deep consequences. It appears that they were successful, because "they arose and filled all the land of Israel with Torah."

The story of the deaths of the disciples may not be well-placed in the context of Akiva's last years, but there is no shortage of stories about his final days. Not surprisingly, the story of his death has occasioned a considerable amount of scholarly research using a variety of methodologies over many years.[31]

A recent close and detailed analysis of the textual traditions around the story by the scholar Paul Mandel reviews many of the complex issues involved in tracing the *textual development* of the story. Just to hint at the complications: the story appears in one version in the Jerusalem Talmud (an early text from the Land of Israel), another in the standard printed edition of the Babylonian Talmud (a later text, obviously from Babylonia), and in still other versions in various manuscripts of the Babylonian Talmud that differ from the printed text. I concentrate on the most well-known and oft-repeated version of the story—the one that appears in the traditional printed edition of the Babylonian Talmud. I then touch briefly on another tradition about the narrative.

The Babylonian Talmud, of course, is structured as a kind of vast (and unruly) commentary on the Mishnah, and the famous tale of the death of Akiva appears there in the context of a discussion of an important passage from the Mishnah:

> A person is required to bless God for evil just as one blesses God for good, as it is written, "And you shall love the Lord your God with all your heart, with all your soul, and with all your might" (Deuteronomy 6:5).
>
> "With all your heart"—with both of your impulses, the good impulse and the bad impulse.
>
> "With all your soul"—even if He takes away your soul [your life].
>
> "With all your might"—with all your wealth.
>
> m. Berakhot "Blessings" 9:5

Here the Mishnah is glossing the opening verses of what came to be known as the central credo of Judaism, the Shema. The words "And you shall love the Lord your God" immediately follow the cry in Deuteronomy 6:4 of *Shema Yisrael*, "Hear O Israel, the Lord is our God, the Lord is One." Observant Jews recite the Shema liturgically twice a day, in the morning and evening prayer services; upon going to sleep; and at a variety of other occasions, including, if one is granted the opportunity, at the time of one's death.[32]

"With all your heart" is understood to encompass what the rabbis viewed as both sides of human beings' dual nature. The "evil impulse" probably misconstrues what they had in mind because "evil" not only refers to acting in a malevolent way, but also includes competitiveness and sexuality—things that the rabbis do not view as essentially "bad"; indeed the rabbis assert that without the evil impulse the world could not be sustained or developed. A better way of understanding the concepts would be to view the "evil impulse" as the id and the "good impulse" as the superego of Sigmund Freud. A world of id without superego would be destructive; one with superego but no id would be bland and stagnant. One needs to love God, the rabbis are saying, with both sides of one's nature.

The interpretation in the text of the word "might" is self-explanatory: one loves God through all one's financial resources —using one's wealth to do good in the world. It is the passage about "all your soul" that is most crucial to our investigation. *Nefesh*, the Hebrew word usually translated as "soul," is understood to stand for one's very life. Even if God takes away one's life, one still must love God.

It is a puzzling passage to be sure. What would it mean to proclaim one's love of God if God took away one's life? And in what way would God be responsible for one's death? The most obvious answer would be that since the rabbis viewed God as the source of all experience, *any* event could be seen as emanating from God. This is not to say that the rabbis saw no place for human agency; indeed, famously in a statement attributed to Rabbi Akiva we read the paradoxical lines, "Everything is foreseen, but free will is given" (m. Avot "Fathers" 3:18).

But the story of God's hand in Akiva's death, as I will argue, may have another side to it as well, beyond a generalized sense that God watches over *all* events.

First let us look at the story. In the Babylonian Talmud the tale begins by laying out the circumstances that led up to his tragic end. It begins with Akiva echoing the Mishnah's commentary on the Shema:[33]

Rabbi Akiva said: "With all your soul"—even if He takes away your soul.

Our rabbis taught: Once the evil kingdom issued a decree forbidding the Jews to occupy themselves with Torah. Pappus ben Yehudah came and found Rabbi Akiva gathering crowds together in public and occupying himself with the Torah. He said to him: "Akiva, aren't you afraid of the kingdom?"

Akiva replied: "I will tell you a parable. To what can this situation be compared: A fox was once walking alongside of a river and saw swarms of fish going from place to place. He said to them: 'From what are you fleeing?'

"The fish replied: 'From the nets that people throw to catch us.'

"The fox said to them: 'Would you like to come up on the dry land so that you and I can live together in the same way that my ancestors lived with your ancestors?'

"They replied: 'Are you really the one that they call the cleverest of animals? You're not clever—you're a fool! If we are afraid in the place in which we live, how much more would we be afraid in the place in which we would die!'"

Akiva continued: "So it is with us. Now we sit and occupy ourselves with Torah. If this is our situation when we sit and occupy ourselves with Torah—of which it is written, 'For it is your life and the length of your days' (Deuteronomy 30:20)—how much worse off will we be if we go and treat Torah as worthless!"

It is said: In just a few days afterward, Rabbi Akiva was taken and put into prison, and Pappus ben Yehudah was also taken and imprisoned next to him.

Akiva said to him: "Pappus, what brought you here?"

He replied: "Happy are you, Rabbi Akiva, that you have been taken for occupying yourself with Torah! Woe to Pappus who has been taken for busying himself with worthless things!"

b. Berakhot 61b

The "evil kingdom" in this story obviously refers to the Roman rule in Eretz Yisrael. The Roman government has issued a ban on Jews "occupying themselves" with Torah, a rabbinic phrase that generally connotes the teaching and learning of Torah and may also include performing the practices of Jewish religious life—the mitzvot. When are these events supposed to have occurred? Rabbinic sources, of course, do not conform to the niceties of modern historical scholarship, so it is not easy to determine the precise time frame intended by this story. Did a ban on Torah study precede the Bar Kokhba War, or did such a ban come into play only as part of Hadrian's decrees after the war had ended? Most scholars today would agree with the statement that the main cause of the Bar Kokhba Revolt "was the rebuilding of Jerusalem as a pagan city called Aelia Capitolina, with a pagan temple within the city," and not a ban on Jewish religious practices.[34] Thus it would seem that the story of Akiva's death, at least within the mythic calendar of rabbinic literature, is meant to follow the *end* of the Bar Kokhba Revolt, and his execution has nothing to do with his supporting the revolt but rather his defying the ban against "occupying oneself" with Torah.

Was there an actual historical ban on teaching and studying Torah? Seth Schwartz points out that we see the embellishment of stories about these persecutions in later rabbinic traditions, including "the prohibition of practicing or even teaching Jewish law on pain of death."[35] The ban on circumcision is the only one that is confirmed in nonrabbinic—that is, Roman—sources. But the idea of a ban on Torah has come down to us through tradition, and even if the real historical reckoning is murky, these stories operate in a context that accepts such a proscription.

Akiva's decision to teach Torah in public—which clearly is meant by his "gathering crowds together"—is perplexing. Doesn't he realize that he thus makes himself vulnerable to punishment? It flies in the face of rabbinic tradition, which generally privileges protecting oneself over placing one's life in danger. The Mishnah, for example, states that during a "time of danger" (understood to be during these Hadrianic bans) a man walking to perform the mitzvah of circumcision should keep the circumcision knife hidden from view (m. Shabbat "Sabbath" 19:1) so that he does not endanger himself by violating the prohibition of circumcision by the Roman government. And even more relevant to our case is the recollection of Rabbi Yehudah using the same "time of danger" phrase:

> Once during a time of danger we carried a Torah scroll from a courtyard onto a roof, from the roof into a courtyard, and from the courtyard into an enclosed space in order to read from it.
>
> b. Eruvin "Blendings" 91a

So why does Akiva, in light of these cautions about placing oneself in danger, decide to bring down the wrath of the government upon himself by teaching Torah in public? Akiva's answer to this question is told in the form of a parable—a type of literature that is well-represented in rabbinic sources.

The parable of the fox and fish is one of the most well-known in rabbinic literature. It is quoted often and retold in children's books and textbooks; nonetheless, its meaning is a bit less clear than what appears at first. What does the water stand for, who is the fox, who are the fish, and who are the people who are casting the nets to catch the fish? The latter "characters"—the fishermen—are rarely discussed, in fact. Daniel Boyarin tries to take account of them and in doing so gives us an inventive, though perhaps not entirely convincing, reading. Viewing the parable in the light of what happens to Akiva and Pappus later in the story, Boyarin suggests: "Both the Jewish 'fish' and the Roman 'fox' end up being hunted and caught by the 'men.' The fox, however, now confesses to the fish that he is in worse shape than they, for his death is meaningless, while theirs is momentous."[36] But Boyarin's interpretation doesn't entirely fit: in the parable the men do not capture the fox; they seem interested only in the fish.

Boyarin seems to understand the fish as the Jews, the fox as Pappus, and the fishermen as the Romans. In his view this is "a story of contention over martyrdom between Rabbinic and Christian Jews. . . . Jews who have abandoned their traditional practice by becoming Christians end up in greater danger than they were in to start with."[37]

A more conventional interpretation makes a good deal more sense to me. The fish are the Jews, the fox stands for the Romans, and the fishermen? Well, they are just characters in the parable with no analogy to the parable's "solution." These tales are not precise allegories; they are less formal than that. The fox is tempting the fish to give up their habitat and join him on the land where once their ancestors lived comfortably together. The Jews by analogy must resist the temptation of the offer made by the Romans: perhaps there was a time that the Jews and the Romans lived peacefully together—before the Bar Kokhba Revolt; is that what is being alluded to? But the fish are doubly in danger: first because the fox may be very pleased to eat the fish once they come out of the water (is a parallel to Jewish assimilation to Roman ways being suggested here?); and second because fish cannot live without being in their natural element, namely, for Jews, the environment of learning Torah, even if there is no Roman fox waiting to gobble them up.

In "times of danger," some may choose to go underground; but, Akiva's parable asserts, others need to stand up for an idea, indeed for the core idea of rabbinic Judaism: without Torah, the Jews might as well not survive. To die for doing something meaningful, something important, is considerably different from dying for busying oneself, as Pappus did, with "worthless things." It is not accidental that the unnamed author of this story uses the exact same Hebrew root (*batal*) when Akiva warns that we must not treat the Torah as "worthless" and when Pappus confesses that his life has been misspent with that which is "worthless."

The legend of Pappus and Akiva serves as the introduction and backdrop to the story of Akiva's death. Akiva has been arrested and imprisoned. The classic accounts give us very little background to these events. Where was he teaching? Where was the prison? Where was the execution? Interestingly, a wide variety of writings about the death of Akiva all state without hesitation that he was executed in the city of Caesarea. But none of the *classical* sources mentions that location. Louis Finkelstein tells us that Akiva was captured and later "transferred to a prison in distant Caesarea," but he gives us no source for this information.[38] No rabbinic tale gives the location of the prison, nor where he was when he was "captured."

Caesarea is certainly not a bad guess for the site of his execution. From around 6 CE and onward that city was the seat of the Roman government in Palestine, and it had an outdoor amphitheater of the sort the Romans used for games, gladiatorial battles, and executions.[39] (Today it is an excavated tourist site.) But in fact, the only rabbinic source that connects Akiva's death to Caesarea is a rather late (ca. ninth century CE) text, the midrash on Proverbs, where we read almost the opposite narrative. In this text Akiva's loyal aide-de-camp Rabbi Joshua HaGarsi is visited by the prophet Elijah, who tells him that Akiva has died. Joshua and Elijah go to the prison where Akiva had been kept, and there they find the jailor asleep and Akiva lying lifeless on his bed. The two men then transport Akiva's body *to* Caesarea for burial.

But no matter where the story's events are set geographically, the tragic endgame plays itself out. The opening lines ("Rabbi Akiva said: 'With all your soul'—even if He takes away your soul") are exemplified in the second part of the story.

Immediately following Pappus's exclamation about "worthless things" the story continues:

> At the hour when Rabbi Akiva was taken out for execution, it was the time for the recital of the Shema. Thus while they were combing his flesh with iron combs, he was accepting upon himself the yoke of the kingdom of heaven.
>
> His students said to him: "Our master, even at this point?"
>
> He said to them: "All my days I have been troubled by this verse [and its proper interpretation], 'with all your soul'—even if He takes away your soul. I said: When will I have the opportunity of fulfilling this? Now that I have the opportunity shall I not fulfill it?"
>
> [In reciting the Shema] he prolonged saying the final word "One" of "Hear O Israel, the Lord is our God, the Lord is One" until his soul departed while saying "One."
>
> A heavenly voice went forth and proclaimed: "Happy are you, Rabbi Akiva, that your soul has departed with the word 'One'!"
>
> b. Berakhot 61b

The judgment of the heavenly voice[40] does not end the story, however. Akiva may be blessed that his life ended with the Oneness of God on his lips, but the ministering angels, watching this scene from above, cry out to God in consternation, "This is Torah and this is its reward!?" How can the great and learned Akiva suffer such a terrible end at the hands of these wicked men? God answers them by saying that Akiva will have eternal life—an answer that is meant to assuage the angels' distress. Then for a second time a heavenly voice is heard, proclaiming, "Happy are you, Rabbi Akiva, that you are invited to the life of the world to come" (b. Berakhot 61b).

Since, as we have seen, classical Jewish tradition establishes two times during the day in which the Shema is to be said—

during the morning and the evening prayers—it appears that Akiva's execution takes place during one of those times, most likely early in the morning. His end is a particularly gruesome one, as his body is raked by iron combs. The story tells us that "he was accepting upon himself the yoke of the kingdom of heaven." This phrase has a specific meaning in classic rabbinic literature: in reciting the first section of the Shema, one takes upon oneself this "yoke"—meaning that the recitation of the Shema is a personal assertion that the only true king is God and God alone.[41] Akiva is in essence doing two things: he is expressing his religious commitment and at the same time rejecting the legitimacy of the Roman kingdom for the kingdom of God. The political statement goes hand in hand with Akiva's spiritual vision, and our story subtly reinforces this by using the same Hebrew word, *malkhut*, for the "kingdom" of heaven as it does when it describes the "evil kingdom" at the beginning of our story. One kingdom stands for all that is right in the world, and the other for all that is wicked.

The most perplexing line in the story is the expression of surprise from Akiva's students: "Our master, even at this point?" What are they asking him? The most obvious sense of their comment is that they hear him reciting the Shema and cannot believe that in the midst of all his suffering he can bring himself to say those words. Are they surprised because of the enormous act of willpower that the recitation would take given those terrible circumstances? The story as I have translated it comes from the standard printed edition of the Talmud, but another, related understanding of the students' question can be seen in Paul Mandel's careful analysis of the manuscript versions of the Talmud.[42]

In one manuscript tradition the text does not read, as the printed edition does, "he was accepting upon himself the yoke of the kingdom of heaven," but rather, "he was concentrating his mind in preparation to accept upon himself the kingdom of heaven." In other words, the students were amazed that under these circumstances Akiva was doing more than a *rote* recitation of the words of the Shema; he was in fact applying full intentionality to the act. At that they are astonished.

One advantage of this version is that it solves a question that has often perplexed commentators: How is it possible that Akiva interrupts his recitation of the Shema to speak with his students when such a break is a clear violation of traditional Jewish law that one must say this prayer without interruption? But no matter which version one subscribes to—the traditional printed text or the manuscript tradition that Mandel calls "Version A"—the main explanation of the students' question remains the same: they are amazed by Akiva's ability to speak those words.

There is, however, another way that we might read this interaction. It is possible that the students are amazed at the nature of the *religious* statement that Akiva is making. Perhaps what they are saying is something along these lines: "Rabbi, even at this point when you are being tortured to death, how is it possible that you can still be proclaiming God's greatness?" In other words, the students may be asking their own version of what the angels cry out in the coda to the story: "This is Torah and this is its reward!?"

But if this is indeed the students' question, Akiva does not answer it. Instead, in the moment of death he does what he has done his entire career—he gives them an interpretation of Torah. Akiva dies, in Michael Fishbane's lovely phrase, in "exegetical ecstasy . . . fulfilling a verse of Scripture."[43]

The Jerusalem Talmud has a different version of these events, in all likelihood an earlier one:

> Rabbi Akiva was being prosecuted by the evil Turnus Rufus when the time came for the recitation of the Shema. Rabbi Akiva began to recite the Shema and laughed.

Turnus Rufus said to him: "Old man, old man! Are you a sorcerer or someone who scoffs at sufferings?"

Akiva replied: "May you perish! I am neither a sorcerer nor one who scoffs at sufferings. But my whole life I have recited the verse 'You shall love the Lord your God with all your heart and with all your soul and with all your might' (Deuteronomy 6:5). I have loved Him with all my heart; I have loved Him with all my wealth; but I have never been tested with fulfilling 'all my soul.' And now that 'all my soul' has arrived for me—as the time for the reciting of the Shema has now come—I will not miss the opportunity to do it. For this reason do I recite it and laugh." Akiva did not get to finish the Shema when his soul departed.[44]

> y. Berakhot 9:5 (also y. Sotah
> "The Suspected Adulteress" 5:7)

Turnus Rufus, as we saw in chapter 3, is the Hebrew appellation for the historical figure Tinneius Rufus, Roman governor of Palestine for a short period around the time of Akiva's death. We see certain elements of the later and more familiar story from the Babylonian Talmud in this earlier recounting. But, as Mandel emphasizes, as much as this story presents a similar reading of the interpretation of the "all my soul" line from Deuteronomy, it has a very different focus. Akiva here, according to Mandel, turns the "simple act of reciting the Shema into *political drama:* Akiva's amusement and joy at being able to perform this act at the very moment that he is being tried becomes a weapon against the ruthless governor."[45] But what is missing from this version and what the Babylonian Talmud adds to the tale is the interaction with Akiva's students. In adding this, the Babylonian Talmud creates the enduring image for all time of Akiva as "the teacher *par excellence*, practicing now, at the culmination of his life, what he has preached to his students 'all his days.'"[46]

What is Akiva teaching them? First, he exemplifies by his

actions that the requirement to say the Shema at its proper time is incumbent on everyone, no matter the circumstances; second, he teaches that the interpretation of the Shema's phrase "with all your soul" *does* mean you are required to bless God even if your very life is taken; and finally he shows that to love God means "to bless God for evil just as one blesses God for good," as we saw in the original discussion in the Mishnah with which we began this story.

I have said that the issue of God's role in the death of Akiva goes beyond the simple theological position that God is responsible for all the events of the world. It also means that Akiva dies because he is intent on teaching God's Torah to Israel and in breaking the Romans' ban. Thus it is his intense connection to God that is at least partially responsible for the terrible end that he meets. This is perhaps what lies behind the angels' lament—where is the justice when a man suffers and dies precisely because he is fulfilling what God has asked of him? It is the problem of "theodicy"—where is God's justice in an unjust and evil world? In this case, the angels get an answer: "Happy are you, Rabbi Akiva, that you are invited to the life of the world to come."

To modern ears this may not seem like a satisfactory answer, but it is the classic religious response to the theodicy problem, and for the rabbis it must have offered some comfort. Their assurance about an afterlife, "a world to come" in some form or another, was part of their worldview.

But Akiva's afterlife was guaranteed in more tangible ways in "this world." The death of Akiva became the prime model for later Jewish martyrs: to die with the Shema on their lips, to fulfill the deeper meaning of the Shema's phrase "with all your soul"—these became the markers, in Michael Fishbane's words, "held before the masses in this exhortation to die for the sanctification of God."[47] Nowhere is this more pronounced or influential than in the late Byzantine "Midrash of the Ten Martyrs" (probably dating from the sixth or seventh century CE), which is more commonly known in a poetic version from its place in the traditional Yom Kippur liturgy. This text, usually called by its opening words "*Eleh Ezkerah*" (These I remember), tells the legend of ten sages who are slaughtered during the Hadrianic persecutions.[48] As Fishbane continues, "Although Akiva is but one saint among many, his heroic death decisively influenced the portrayal of others," even down to the "promise of an eternal reward in heaven."[49] Akiva was the ultimate example of Jewish self-sacrifice, and his "afterlife" lived on throughout the millennia in the memory of his people.

——————◆◆◆◆——————

The Afterlife of Akiva

To DIE saying the Shema, to fight against attempts to abrogate the study of Torah, to fulfill your mission as teacher even at the point of death—these are legacies handed down through the powerful narrative of Akiva's last moments. But Akiva's afterlife—that is, his place in the consciousness of the Jewish people—goes beyond his tragic death. He has lived on as the hero figure of rabbinic Judaism in many ways.

To begin with, we have his teachings, or, to be more precise, we have the teachings *attributed* to him in our classic texts. Akiva's name appears more than a thousand times in the Babylonian Talmud alone. Of course we cannot with confidence say that every statement made in Rabbi Akiva's name was really spoken by him. The teachings of rabbis from the Tannaitic period (that is, early traditions) are often quoted in later sources such as the Babylonian Talmud, which was edited some three hundred to four hundred years after the Mishnah. Richard Kal-

min has put it well: "During the course of transmission many
of these statements were altered, emended, and completed in
subtle or not so subtle ways, such that a statement's attribution
to a Tannaitic Rabbi cannot be accepted at face value. How
much, if anything, of the statement is Tannaitic? Has it been
doctored by later generations? Is it an invention by later generations based on false assumptions about attitudes in a much
earlier time?"[1] And I suspect that as Akiva's fame grew in the
generations after his death, his name became associated with
comments simply because of his great prestige. But later Jewish
history has offered a judgment on the Akivan legacy no matter what the "real" Akiva may or may not have said: these are
teachings that endure across the ages as being his.

Probably no statement attributed to Akiva is more well-
known and more associated with him than this one: of the
verse "love your neighbor as yourself" (Leviticus 19:18), Rabbi
Akiva said, "This is the great principle of the Torah." It has
even made it into a popular Hebrew song, "Rabbi Akiva Said."
The utterance is usually quoted as a stand-alone statement,
but as it appears in rabbinic literature, it is actually part of a debate between Akiva and Ben Azzai. The full discussion appears
like this:

> "Love your neighbor as yourself" (Leviticus 19:18)
> Rabbi Akiva said: This is the great principle of the Torah.
> Ben Azzai said: "This is the record of Adam's line"
> (Genesis 5:1)—This principle is even greater than that.
>
> y. Nedarim "Vows" 9:4 (also in Sifra on Leviticus 19:18)

This discussion, appearing in parallel versions in two early texts
—the Jerusalem Talmud and the midrash on Leviticus called
Sifra—is a debate about defining the most important tenet in
the Torah.

Akiva's statement is clear: the most important thing that

the Torah teaches is to "love your neighbor as yourself." But what is Ben Azzai trying to say with his odd quotation from Genesis? As is often the case in these texts, it is worthwhile to look at the whole biblical context of the quoted verses. What Ben Azzai is really after is the way that the verse continues: "This is the record of Adam's line—When God created man, He made him in the likeness of God; male and female He created them" (Genesis 5:1–2).

For Ben Azzai the important point is that all human beings are created in God's image, and therefore no one person is superior to another; for Akiva the key principle in the Torah is the requirement to love one's fellow human beings. Both sides of the argument have merit. There is something appealing about Akiva's elevation of the emotion of love, and at the same time there is something comforting in Ben Azzai's concept of a just society. What is interesting and somewhat surprising is that this is one of the rare rabbinic debates in which Akiva appears to be bested, or at least Ben Azzai has the last word. One suspects that this troubled some authorities because of the strength of Akiva's reputation. When the same debate is reported in another midrash, it comes out differently:

> Ben Azzai said: "This is the record of Adam's line" (Genesis 5:1)—This is the great principle of the Torah.
> Rabbi Akiva said: "Love your neighbor as yourself" (Leviticus 19:18)—*This* is the great principle of the Torah!
>
> Genesis Rabbah 24:7

The midrash here seems to be working on making sure that Akiva gets the winning comment, but it is hardly necessary. Even though Ben Azzai might be seen as the winner of the debate in the Jerusalem Talmud and the Sifra, it is the Akivan ideal of loving one's fellow human beings that has come down to us as the remembered essential principle of the rabbis.

The debate about the "great principle" of Torah—meaning in the rabbis' terms a dispute about the core commitment of Judaism—might be said to have a companion piece in another discussion about a fundamental element in the rabbinic world-view. The rabbis were taken up by the two deepest matters of Jewish religious life: study of Torah on the one hand and the "practice" of Judaism—performing the various commandments outlined in the Torah (and in the rabbinic interpretation of Torah)—on the other. Here too Akiva has a major role:

> It once happened that Rabbi Tarfon and the elders were gathered together in the upper story of Nitza's house in Lod, when this question was raised before them: Which is greater, study or practice?
>
> Rabbi Tarfon answered: Practice is greater.
>
> Rabbi Akiva answered: Study is greater.
>
> Then they all answered: Study is greater for it leads to practice.

> b. Kiddushin "Betrothal" 40b[2]

We don't have any information about who Nitza was, though his "upper story" meeting room is mentioned in another talmudic tractate.[3] Nitza, we can assume, was wealthy enough to have a house with an upper story and devout enough to let his house be used for rabbinic meetings and discussions.

The Hebrew word translated as "gathered together" (*m'subin*) also has the meaning of "reclining." It is in this sense that it appears in the famous "Four Questions" of the Passover Haggadah to explain that the meal should be eaten while "reclining," not "sitting." Indeed *m'subin* is the term also used when the Haggadah describes the story of Akiva and his four colleagues recounting the story of the Exodus throughout the night, which is understood to be a model of the intense conversation appropriate to the Seder. Early rabbinic literature often uses the word *m'subin* to describe people *gathered* for a formal meal—a "reclining meal" we might say—so perhaps that is what is going on in Nitza's attic room: a dinner conversation that turns into a debate.[4]

The stakes are high in this dispute because it asks whether Judaism is to be a religion fundamentally about the life of the mind or the life of action. Theory or practice? Thinking or deeds? For the rabbis these were matters of great moment.

In the debate reported in the Talmud, neither Rabbi Tarfon nor Rabbi Akiva gives an explanation for his position. The views are stated starkly. The debate ends with "they all answered," whereby the text seems to be saying that it was not just the "elders" who were adjudicating the debate but that Rabbi Tarfon and Rabbi Akiva also joined in with the conclusion. So is this a debate that Akiva has "won"? On the surface it does appear so—between study and deeds, study is said to be more important, which was Akiva's position. But the answer is more complicated because a new element has been introduced into the conclusion. A *reason* is given for the concluding view: "Study is greater *for it leads to practice.*" The conclusion therefore is paradoxical. Study *is* greater, true; but it is greater *because* it leads to practice. In other words, Rabbi Tarfon's position is confirmed after all. If study is important because it leads to practice, then must we not say that practice is greater than study?

I think the real point here is that "all" of them found a way to agree. Akiva could hold the "study" point of view since it is given precedence, but Tarfon can feel that he is vindicated because "practice" is seen to be the purpose of study. What endures from this meeting at Nitza's home is a fundamental tension within Judaism that has played itself out throughout the generations in a variety of ways. Is study meant to be instrumental—aimed at teaching people the proper way to act—as is suggested by the conclusion of our text? Or is study fulfilling some other purpose, even beyond intellectual engagement?

This debate, begun in Akiva's time, has endured throughout the ages.[5]

Investigating voluminous teachings on various topics attributed to Akiva presents significant methodological issues related to attribution and the transmission of traditions. I have highlighted only two rather central matters deeply associated with him in the texts we have just considered. But I would be remiss if I left the impression that Akiva was solely concerned with questions like those we have explored in the texts above, as important as those matters may be. There is another side to Akiva, one that we saw in the story of his ascent in the orchard (chapter 6). This is the Akiva who has been a hero for Jewish mystics throughout history,[6] the Akiva who was intoxicated by the divine, who loved God so much that he went to his death proclaiming that love through saying the Shema—"even if He takes your life."

Akiva's passion, the eros of his connection to God, is reflected in a famous comment attributed to him about the canonical status of the Song of Songs (called in the Christian Bible the Song of Solomon). Was this book of sufficient piety to be included in the Bible? The Song of Songs presented a serious challenge, as it reads like a collection of starkly erotic love poems with no spiritual content at all. What place would such an obviously *secular* book have in the Bible?

In the Mishnah a number of rabbis are disputing the status of Ecclesiastes and the Song of Songs—Rabbi Judah the Patriarch, Rabbi Yose the Galilean, and Rabbi Shimon ben Azzai are all weighing in. Do these two books, they ask, have sacred status?[7] Regarding the Song of Songs Akiva makes an impassioned argument, bringing the discussion to a close:

> Heaven forbid. No person in Israel ever disputed the holiness of the Song of Songs! For all the ages are not equal to

the day when Song of Songs was given to Israel.[8] For all the Writings are sacred but the Song of Songs is the holy of holies—and if there was any dispute, it was only about Ecclesiastes.

m. Yadaim "Hands" 3:5

How the Bible came to be "the Bible" as we know it today—the process known as the canonization of the Bible—is not a simple question. Scholarship today no longer accepts the image of a group of early rabbis gathered together for a few weeks at Rabban Gamaliel's academy in Yavneh and voting up or down on the various books for inclusion or exclusion. Unfortunately for all of us wishing for such a neat, clean story, it appears that the process was a good deal more complex than that, and many of the details are simply unknown.[9]

The report of the debate in rabbinic sources—even though it may not reflect the exact particularities of the canonization process—gives us an insight into Akiva's thinking about this biblical work. For Akiva, the Song of Songs is nothing less than an extended metaphor—not of the love between two human beings, as it seems on the surface, but of the eternal love of God and Israel. Michael Fishbane points out that for Akiva, the Song of Songs "not only bespoke the covenant relationship between Israel and God, it also depicted God in terms even bolder than those reported by the prophet Ezekiel in his vision of the divine chariot. If some of R. Akiva's colleagues had doubts as to the Song's sacred nature, he himself had none. In his view it truly was the holy of holies."[10] An even bolder statement of the importance of the Song of Songs is attributed to Akiva in a late (tenth-century) midrash called Aggadat Shir Ha-Shirim: "Had the Torah not been given, it would have been possible to conduct the world on the basis of the Song of Songs alone."[11] Akiva's association with the Song of Songs, then, is deeply embedded within Jewish tradition, highlighting the emphasis that he placed on love as a central value.

The legacy of Akiva encompasses not only his specific teachings; perhaps even more influential was his vision of the nature of interpretation, a view that helped define the center of Judaism in general and Jewish learning in particular from his time forward. In other words, it was not only the message (or messages) that he communicated through his teachings but the *method* he brought to the enterprise that defined how future generations viewed him.

In Avot de Rabbi Natan there is a passage in which Rabbi Judah the Patriarch reflects on the qualities of some of the rabbis who preceded him by one or two generations. Of Akiva he said, "He was like a well-stocked storehouse." He continued:

> What was Rabbi Akiva like? A worker who took his basket and went outside. When he found wheat, he put it in the basket. When he found barley, he put it in. Spelt—he put it in. Beans—he put them in. Lentils—he put them in. When he came home he sorted out the wheat by itself, the barley by itself, the spelt by itself, the beans by themselves, and the lentils by themselves. This is what Rabbi Akiva did; he made the entire Torah into rings upon rings.
>
> Avot de Rabbi Natan, Version A, chapter 18

It is important to remember that tradition understands Rabbi Judah to be the person who put together the Mishnah, the fundamental text of rabbinic Judaism. In doing so he organized the teachings of the first 150 to 200 years of the culture of the sages. Yet in this text Judah pays tribute to what Akiva did almost a century before the Mishnah. Akiva, like the worker in the parable, came across disorganized, scattered materials—the "food," we might say, that was Torah. He gathered these materials together, but he did more than that: he also sorted them; he took them out of the basket in which they were all jumbled together and figured out a scheme of organization, making "the entire Torah into rings upon rings."

In Rabbi Judah's mind, it appears that there already was a kind of "proto-Mishnah" before the Mishnah came into existence. Judah is paying an enormous compliment to Akiva here. He is close to saying, "What I did, you had already done"— or at least you had already begun. Is this perception true historically? No one has ever discovered the "Mishnah of Rabbi Akiva," but as one scholar has put it, Akiva's "importance for the development of the Mishnah tradition is undoubted."[12] Akiva may be "the father" of our Mishnah, but the particular literary form of *the* Mishnah, as it has come down to us today, cannot be directly attributed to him. Of one thing there is no dispute: in the eyes of tradition, Akiva was the essential figure that allowed the Mishnah we know to come into existence in Rabbi Judah's time.

But I think this text is actually saying something more as well. The Hebrew word *m'varar* that I translated as "sorted" has another, more primary, meaning as well, and in that meaning we have an additional clue to the interpretation of this passage. *M'varer*, from the Hebrew root *b-r-r*, fundamentally means "to make things clear," usually in the intellectual sense of proving or interpreting something. The physical act of sorting a basket of items mixed together is one way of making things clear, but what this text means to suggest, I believe, is that Akiva did more than place various laws and practices into neat categories—as might be assumed from the metaphor of the worker with the produce. Akiva *clarified* the Judaism that had come down to him. He interpreted it, made sense of it, and perhaps most importantly from Rabbi Judah's perspective, he passed that on to Judah and to future generations.

More than an organizer of traditions, Akiva was an *interpreter* of traditions, and his mode of interpretation set the tone for the approach to reading Jewish texts that influenced all of later Jewish religious history. His view was wide-ranging and expansive. It was sometimes outlandish (as in his midrash from the Passover Haggadah about the number of plagues that affected the Egyptians at the time of the Exodus) but filled with imagination.

It was not the only way that the story could have gone; there were other approaches to the study of Torah, but it was Akiva's that ended up enduring. Looking at the differences in the interpretive practices of the early rabbis led the nineteenth-century German Jewish scholar Rabbi David Zvi Hoffmann to suggest that this literature emanated from two different "schools": the school of Rabbi Yishmael and the school of Rabbi Akiva. According to this view, Yishmael and Akiva, who are often described as taking opposing points of view in rabbinic debates, passed on to their students two contrasting modes of thought, terminology, and interpretive strategies. Certain midrashic texts were seen as products of the school of Akiva, others of the school of Yishmael.[13]

Since Hoffmann first suggested the theory of two schools, scholars have debated a series of questions: Are there in fact two schools? If so, how do they differ? Are the interpretative styles as distinctive as one might think by their being categoried as two "schools"? Or are the two approaches more alike than different? And were these two schools truly related to the actual historical figures of Akiva and Yishmael? Some scholars, for example, have accepted the notion of there being two schools but have suggested dropping the nomenclature of "Akivan" or "Yishmaelan" to describe them since it is hard to claim on historical evidence that the two rabbis really initiated two distinctive schools—although it is clear that there *are* two different interpretative approaches at play in the rabbinic sources. Still, the terminology associating these traditions with these two early rabbis has pretty much stuck,[14] which is to say, most scholars continue to use the terms that Hoffmann first introduced despite whether Akiva and Yishmael were in fact responsible for these ongoing traditions.

Most of the writing about the "two schools" is of a highly technical nature focused in particular on two matters: the historical editing and evolution of the works in question, and the interpretative techniques used within the midrashic texts (the "hermeneutics," to use the scholars' favored term).[15] But for our purposes here, how might we look at the ways that these traditions shed light on our portrait of Akiva?

This was a question of great interest, I suspect, when Abraham Joshua Heschel, one of the key Jewish theologians of the twentieth century, wrote a massive work laying out what he saw as the two competing traditions of Akiva and Yishmael.[16] Some academic scholars criticized Heschel's work for failing to distinguish between early and later sources and for taking at face value some of the historical claims emanating from traditional texts. But these criticisms seem to miss the main point of Heschel's work. As Gordon Tucker puts it, Heschel may have "set out here to establish his bona fides as an aficionado of Rabbinic literature, but he certainly does not set out to do meticulous history." Rather, Heschel was interested in seeing Akiva and Yishmael as "eternal paradigms of religious thought that sometimes war with one another, sometimes complement one another, and always challenge and refine one another."[17] The Akiva that Heschel describes is one version of the "legacy Akiva" that comes down to us.

For Heschel, the contrast between Akiva and Yishmael is a contrast of theologies and a consequent divergence of methods in interpreting the Torah. Akiva, as Heschel portrays him, is always looking for the hidden meanings in Torah; Yishmael seeks to focus on the less dramatic, "plainer" sense of the biblical text being discussed.[18]

In many ways Heschel's book is an attempt to rehabilitate

the image of Rabbi *Yishmael*, to argue that—as he was devoted to "cool analysis" with "no concern for hidden things"—he had lost out to Akiva's pursuit of the mysteries of Torah. Akiva is the glamorous and exciting figure in Heschel's view. "In the end," writes Heschel, "it was the approach of Rabbi Akiva that conquered the hearts of Israel and was absorbed into its heritage. It is so woven and intermeshed in the lexicon of Jewish thought that one hardly perceives it as a distinct force."[19]

There is no doubt that Heschel's binary categorization of the two rabbinic figures overstates the case to make the contrast. But in the arena of understanding the interpretative methods of the two schools, Heschel is not so far from views that we can find in contemporary scholarship. In his meticulous analysis of the two schools, Menahem Kahana concludes that indeed, "Yishmael's midrash is generally more moderate than R. Akiva's, and his expositions are also less distant from the simple meaning of the verse." He objects to Heschel's characterization of Yishmael as "a rationalist who vigorously opposed esoteric expositions of the Torah and matters that cannot be attained by the intellect." But Kahana goes on to talk about Akiva's "far-reaching way of expounding" while Yishmael "opposed the minute exposition of biblical verses practiced by R. Akiva."[20] Contemporary scholarship, then, would chart these differences as significant though considerably less pronounced than Heschel's presentation.

The single most dramatic example of the rabbis' own understanding of Rabbi Akiva's interpretative radicalism can be found in one of the greatest of all Akiva stories:

> Rav Judah said in the name of Rav, When Moses ascended on high to receive the Torah, he found the Holy One, blessed be He, sitting and attaching little crowns to the letters. Moses said to him: "Master of the Universe, what is holding you back [from giving the Torah]?"

God answered, "There will be a man in the future, at the end of a number of generations, and Akiva ben Joseph is his name. He will interpret heaps and heaps of laws from just the tips of these crowns."

Moses said, "Master of the Universe, show him to me!"

God replied, "Turn around!"

Moses went and sat down in the back, behind eight rows [of students]. But he did not understand what they were saying and he was distressed. When they came upon a certain matter, the students asked Rabbi Akiva: "Master, from where do you know this?" and he said to them, "It is a law given to Moses at Sinai," and Moses was comforted.

Moses returned and came before the Holy One, blessed be He, and said, "Master of the Universe, you have a man like that and you're giving the Torah through *me*!" God replied, "Quiet! This is what I have decided."

b. Menahot "Meal Offerings" 29b

Moses has gone up onto Mount Sinai to receive the Torah and finds God working, as it were, on the finishing touches of the document. In the traditional calligraphy of a Torah scroll, eight different letters in the Hebrew alphabet have special ornamentations, here called "crowns." Instead of moving forward with giving the Torah, God is waiting until he finishes this calligraphic work. Moses is astonished. The entire revelation of Torah is being delayed because of this small matter!

But God has a response. This, God says, is not a mere affectation or aesthetic nicety. In the future a man named Akiva ben Joseph (one of the rare times in rabbinic literature that Akiva's full name is used) will come along who will be able to use these little crowns to interpret "heaps and heaps" of laws. Moses is amazed and longs to see this extraordinary person. God accommodates his request by putting Moses into a kind of time machine to the future. All of a sudden Moses is sitting in the back of Akiva's classroom. It is a stunning narrative move, surprising to find in a talmudic text. But the time travel element is clearly intentional; the Talmud scholar Jeffrey Rubenstein points out that the phrase "Turn around" could also be translated "Turn to the future."[21]

Sitting in that class, Moses is distressed. He understands nothing that is being said. This is a remarkable story in many ways—the time travel, the pairing of Moses and Akiva, the role of God—but nothing is quite as extraordinary as the moment when Moses becomes depressed by his inability to understand the discussion. It is only when Akiva cites Moses's authority that Moses is able to revive himself. Not only is Akiva asserting the importance of Moses, but it is no accident that the text has him use the traditional phrase "a law given to Moses at Sinai"—at the exact moment in the midrash when Moses is standing on Sinai about to receive the Torah.

What does it mean that Moses cannot understand the future debates surrounding the very Torah that he is about to receive from God? Moses is so distressed that he wants God to give the Torah through Akiva, not through him. But God will not relent, nor will God explain the reasoning behind that decision: "Shut up," God essentially tells him, "I've made my decision."

One of the most extraordinary things about this story is that the rabbis who composed it show how well aware they were of the necessary evolution of Torah interpretation over time. Even Moses—the greatest of all the prophets, the person closest to God's revelation—even Moses will not be able to understand the way that Torah interpretation grows over time. Rubenstein, in his close reading of the story, puts it well. The storytellers here are trying to deal with "the gap between the original revelation on Mount Sinai and the contemporary Torah of the rabbis of the Talmudic period. The storytellers are keenly aware that Torah has expanded and developed as each Rabbinic generation has added interpretations, legal pronouncements and explanations to the corpus of tradition. . . . How can a tradition be part of *Torat Moshe*, the 'Torah of Moses,' and at the same time be attributed to later sages?" According to Rubenstein, the storytellers' solution, the concept that comforts Moses in his depression, is "that the expanded and developed Torah of the Rabbinic era somehow inheres in the original Torah revealed to Moses."[22]

The true heroic figure in the story is Akiva. It is Akiva whose imagination sets the tone for the future development of Torah. Perhaps the reason that God does not answer Moses's question is to protect Moses from the knowledge that the Torah that Moses delivered to Israel, the Torah that was at the heart of his life's work, will eventually change, will become unrecognizable even to Moses.

Interestingly there is no text in the rabbinic corpus in which Akiva (or anyone else) uses the crowns on the letters to interpret "heaps and heaps" of anything. It is a literary flourish, a hyperbole aimed at making the larger point about Akiva's status. The story, in the words of Azzan Yadin-Israel, brings together two themes:

> the inherently mysterious Torah; and the gifted interpreter capable of uncovering its secrets. The mysteries of the Torah are, the narrative informs us, located in the crowns of the letters. These graphic flourishes are not part of the language of the Torah, and their interpretation indicates that Rabbi Akiva is able to derive meaning even from non-semantic aspects of the text. They are in other words, oracular markers that are . . . meaningless to all but "an interpreter gifted with divine insight." Clearly, Rabbi Akiva is this interpreter, the reader for whom the Torah is intended; he is—ontologically —*the* reader of Torah, since God composed the work with Rabbi Akiva in mind.[23]

As remarkable as this story is up to this point, its conclusion is almost as extraordinary:

Moses said to God: "Master of the Universe, you have shown me his Torah, now show me his reward."

God said: "Turn around," and Moses turned around and saw them weighing out Akiva's flesh in the marketplace.

"Master of the Universe," Moses said, "this is Torah and this is the reward!?"

God replied: "Quiet! This is what I have decided."

b. Menahot 29b

Moses asks God a question once again, and once again God does not answer. But here the question is a good deal darker. Moses has received another glimpse into the future and has been brought to the execution of Akiva. We are given a gruesome detail that did not appear in the other stories of Akiva's death: the flesh that the iron combs had ripped from Akiva's body is now being sold in the market. The question that Moses asks is precisely the same question the angels asked in the Babylonian Talmud's version of Akiva's death: "This is Torah and this is its reward!?"

There, God gave a different answer: Akiva is invited into the "world to come." He is promised an afterlife as compensation. But here, there is no recompense. It is a stark "Quiet!" from God—a response that feels particularly resonant for us today: there is no answer to the suffering of the righteous, and the promise of the world to come offers small comfort. This text seems to be saying that even for the greatest of rabbinic heroes the mystery of death and suffering is somehow beyond human comprehension, locked in the mind of God and inaccessible to any of us.

What, in the end, can we say about Rabbi Akiva? Throughout this book I have tried to keep in mind the words of the novelist Margaret Atwood in the epigraph: "There's the story, then there's the real story, then there's the story of how the story came to be told. Then there's what you leave out of the story. Which is part of the story too."[24] Akiva's story is told in rabbinic literature through a variety of sources and in a variety of ways. Yet the fact that the traditions handed down to us have been shaped by the anonymous editors who lived after Akiva's time—well after his time in most cases—does not diminish the story. It only means that we can never know the "real" story, just as surely as we can never know where Akiva is buried.

I have tried to tell Akiva's story along with at least some of what we know about "how the story came to be told." What we have received from our sources surely is only part, perhaps even a small part, of all the stories that once upon a time were told about this hero. What was left out, we cannot know, but that too is part of the biography and part of the mystery of his life.

As in any story of a remarkable individual, we find in Akiva's life complexities and even some contradictions. Yet some things stand out clearly. First, his sheer intellectual brilliance. This is a theme in both of the origin stories—whether Akiva is the father beginning to learn the aleph-bet alongside his son and going on to master the entire corpus of texts and "uproot" his masters; or whether he is the young impoverished shepherd following his wife's advice to go learn Torah. We see his peers astonished by his abilities, and perhaps a bit envious as well. Yet with all his talent, he still learns at the feet of his own teachers —he "serves the sages" and is humbled by what he has yet to learn. There is Akiva's remarkable mixture of pride and humility, as he dismantles the "mountain" that came before him on the one hand yet tells the brother of Dosa ben Harkinas that he has not even attained the rank of shepherds on the other. And perhaps there is an old injury that stays with him; lacking an ancestry of either learning or wealth, he is conscious, at least in his early years, of the social status that he does not have.

In some of the sources we see a profound connection to his wife, as he honors her and recognizes what she has sacrificed for him. In later years he finally gives her the life of comfort that he feels she deserves, but much of their life together remains unknown to us. It appears that he has known tragedy in his life—the hazy references to the deaths of children, the strange plague that kills his students—and his life ends with terrifying torture. But he becomes the great figure of a heroic death, an exemplar for the ages; he is the model for Jewish mystics, ascending to God's hidden chamber and returning to life unscathed; and in his defense of the Song of Songs and in his argument with Ben Azzai over the fundamental teaching of the Torah, he becomes the great advocate for love in the rabbinic tradition.

This is, at least in part, the outline of the "story" of Akiva; its relationship to what Atwood calls "the real story" will never be known. Nor, to my mind, does it much matter. For me this idea is best summed up in the essay on Moses by the great early Zionist thinker Ahad Ha'am (the penname of Asher Ginzberg, 1856–1927). Ahad Ha'am's "Moses," in the words of his biographer, "represented his most coherent attempt to sketch out the meaning of authentic leadership in Jewish culture," and it captures quite beautifully an idea that applies well to the story of Akiva, that "what ultimately mattered was not necessarily what was historically accurate but what entered the historical consciousness";[25] that is, what ends up being truly important is the shared memory of people down through the ages, no matter what the historical facts may have been. Ahad Ha'am put this idea, regarding Moses, in lyrical prose: There are times, he wrote, when

> I see learned men digging around in the dust of ancient books and manuscripts to raise from their graves the heroes of history in their true form. . . . but it seems to me that they are liable to overrate the value of their discoveries. They don't want to see the simple fact that not every archeological truth is a historical truth. . . .

Did Moses really exist? Did his life and actions really correspond to what has been handed down to us? . . . There are many questions like these but in my heart I wipe them away in an instant with a short and simple answer: *This* Moses, this man of the ancient past . . . is of no concern to anybody but the antiquarians. . . . For we have *another* Moses, our Moses, whose image is fixed in the hearts of our people from generation to generation and whose influence on our national life has never ceased, from days of old to the present.[26]

So too with Akiva who, interestingly, is often associated with Moses in rabbinic literature. The Akiva who has come down to us through stories and teachings is the image "fixed in the hearts of our people from generation to generation," and as much as we have important things to learn from scholars, ideas that will help clarify his context and make sense of the sources that we have inherited, the Akiva of the imagination, of "historical consciousness," will continue to live on. His afterlife is assured.

Early on in my work on this book a wise friend asked me an interesting question: "I know Finkelstein's Akiva," he said to me, "and I know Heschel's Akiva, and others as well. What I'm wondering about is what is *your* Akiva?" It was a question that I wasn't ready to answer when he asked it. But it was not far from my mind during the next few years as I worked on this project.

Of course, there are many Akivas. For some people, I'm sure, the first image that comes to mind is the story of his death. It is enshrined in Jewish liturgy and is the model for martyrdom that sadly has been enacted many times throughout Jewish history. I too have that terrifying picture of Akiva in mind. Second is Akiva the scholar and interpreter—the fertile and innovative reader whose mind, as Heschel put it, "conquered the hearts of Israel." And though one cannot claim that Akiva created this interpretative mode, it has been so deeply associated with his life and teachings across time that he might as well have. And of course I think of him like that as well.

But neither of these two Akivas is the one that stands out for me. When I picture Akiva, mostly I think of him among the sages, part of that small community, that *havurah*, that circle of friends, of teachers and disciples, arguing, conversing, agreeing, and disagreeing, sitting at meals, at prayer, or teaching and learning in small rooms in the homes of the sages or of wealthy friends. That multivocal assembly of voices recognizes Akiva's genius, but he is not the only teacher, and at times he is in fact a student. Disagreement is allowed; indeed it is encouraged.[27] This is where Akiva shines, where his heart sings—in the give-and-take of learning and debate. He may be discussing the Exodus from Egypt with his colleagues until dawn. He may be walking on a hillside overlooking Jerusalem, or comforting Rabbi Joshua after he has been humiliated by Rabban Gamaliel. Or he may be teaching his students while he is in the grasp of the Roman torturers. But he is always part of a community of companions, even the ones with whom he disagrees. Or even when he is being criticized. The Talmud quotes a folk saying that sums it up well. In Aramaic it is "*o hevruta, o mituta*," and a fair English translation would be, "Give me friendship or give me death" (b. Ta'anit "Fast Days" 23a). That is the Akiva who stays with me most of all: a man in the community of the sages, talking about Torah, setting the stage for the future.

NOTES

Introduction

1. In English the name is variously written "Akiva," "Akiba," or even "Aqiba." In recent years the consensus, at least in most scholarly works, seems to have landed on Akiva, and that is the form I use here. Throughout this book, except in citing English-language book titles, I have regularized the spelling to Akiva, even in quotations from sources that use one of the other variants.

2. See the informative description by the historian Shaye Cohen, "The Place of the Rabbi in Jewish Society of the Second Century," in *The Galilee in Late Antiquity* (Jerusalem: Jewish Theological Seminary Press, 1992), 157–74.

3. In her important and exhaustive study, *The Social Structure of the Rabbinic Movement in Roman Palestine* (Tübingen: Mohr Siebeck, 1997), Catherine Hezser writes, "It seems from the first century onwards, the designation 'Rabbi' was used for a Torah teacher who had a circle of disciples" (p. 61).

4. Beth A. Berkowitz, "Reclaiming Halakhah: On the recent

works of Aharon Shemesh," *Association for Jewish Studies (AJS) Review* 35:1, 125–26.

5. The abbreviation CE has generally replaced the Christologically oriented abbreviation AD ("anno Domini," Latin meaning "in the year of our Lord," referring to Jesus). Likewise, BCE, or "before the Common Era," has replaced BC ("before Christ").

6. The word "Mishnah" means "repetition," "recitation," or in sum, "teaching."

7. The Mishnah is written in Hebrew, while much of the Babylonian Talmud is written in Aramaic, a language closely related to Hebrew. Various dialects of Aramaic were used as the lingua franca of the ancient Jewish world, in Palestine and Babylonia.

8. References to pages in the Babylonian Talmud are always given by the number of the "leaf." Each leaf consists of what we could call two pages. The recto side is indicated in English by the letter "a" and the verso by the letter "b," as in "62b."

9. Not surprisingly, there are other terms and other complexities that scholars have adduced, but they are not as relevant to our concerns here. For a useful and clearly written introduction to all of these matters, see Robert Goldenberg, "Talmud," in *Back to the Sources: Reading the Classic Jewish Texts*, ed. Barry W. Holtz (New York: Simon and Schuster, 1984), 129–75.

10. Expansively including what we today might distinguish as civil law, criminal law, and religious practices. The legal literature is *halakhah* (adjective in English: halakhic); the nonlegal parts of rabbinic literature (stories, theological speculation, a good deal of biblical narrative interpretation) is called *aggadah* (aggadic).

11. The abbreviation "R." before a person's name conventionally stands for "Rabbi" or "Rav" (the term for ordination used in Jewish Babylonia). Here, as elsewhere, "ben" is the term for "son of" and is used in the patronymic for Hebrew names. Family names (last names) did not appear until much later in Jewish history.

12. The term "rabban" is synonymous with "rabbi," and most scholars believe that the titles are not meant to indicate any difference in status between the two.

13. Jacob Neusner, "Story and Tradition in Judaism," in *Juda-*

ism: The Evidence of the Mishnah (Chicago: University of Chicago Press, 1981), 310–11.

14. For a description of Fraenkel's method see, Hillel Newman, "Closing the Circle: Yonah Fraenkel, The Talmudic Story, and Rabbinic History," in *How Should Rabbinic Literature Be Read in the Modern World?*, ed. Matthew A. Kraus (Piscataway, NJ: Gorgias, 2006).

15. Newman points out that Fraenkel makes a clear distinction between what he calls "artistic" stories—the stories that Fraenkel focuses on—and "realistic" halakhic stories, stories whose sole purpose was to indicate a practice of a particular rabbi in regard to a point of Jewish law. Ibid., 108.

16. An idea associated with great educational psychologist Jerome Bruner, such as in his classic article "Two Modes of Thought," in *Actual Minds, Possible Worlds* (Cambridge: Harvard University Press, 1987), 11–43.

17. See Rubenstein's *Talmudic Stories: Narrative Art, Composition, and Culture* (Baltimore: Johns Hopkins University Press, 1999); *The Culture of the Babylonian Talmud* (Baltimore: Johns Hopkins University Press, 2003); *Stories of the Babylonian Talmud* (Baltimore: Johns Hopkins University Press, 2010); and a collection of the stories, with short commentaries, aimed at general readers, *Rabbinic Stories* (Mahwah, NJ: Paulist Press, 2002).

18. These include works by scholars writing for other scholars and from a variety of authors aiming at a general reader. These writers include Jacob Neusner and Yonah Fraenkel, as already mentioned, and more recent writers such as Richard Kalmin, Jeffrey Rubenstein, Burton Visotzky, and Daniel Boyarin in the United States; and Admiel Kosmin, Ruth Calderon, Benjamin Lau, and Shulamit Valler in Israel.

19. Ian Scott-Kilvert, *Makers of Rome: Nine Lives by Plutarch* (London: Penguin, 1965), 12.

20. Rubenstein, *Talmudic Stories*, 6.

21. One surprising mention is by St. Jerome (d. 420 CE), who mentions "Akibas" in a list of rabbis in one of his biblical commentaries.

22. The rabbinics scholar Steven Fraade, for example, in his book *From Tradition to Commentary* (Albany: State University of New York Press, 1991), writes: "From shortly after the destruction of the Second Temple (70 CE) until our earliest Rabbinic texts in the third century—precisely that period during which the Rabbinic movement took root and presumably underwent significant development—we do not have a single datable Rabbinic text. Nor do we have much in the way of pertinent archeological or extra-Rabbinic literary evidence. . . . Therefore, we have little way to measure the historical reliability of Rabbinic accounts of the lives and teachings of the sages of that time (the Tannaim)" (p. 72).

23. Louis Finkelstein, *Akiba: Scholar, Saint and Martyr* (Philadelphia: Jewish Publication Society, 1936).

24. Finkelstein, for example, tells us what Akiva's childhood house looked like and how he played games with the other children in the neighborhood; he tells us what Akiva's father was thinking and what his father's occupation was. There are no stories in the rabbinic literature about any of these matters as they specifically relate to Akiva.

25. Milton Steinberg, *As a Driven Leaf* (Springfield, NJ: Behrman House, 1939).

26. Joseph Opatoshu, *The Last Revolt: The Story of Rabbi Akiba*, trans. Moshe Spiegel (Philadelphia: Jewish Publication Society, 1952).

27. Howard Schwartz and Marc Bregman, *The Four Who Entered Paradise* (Northvale, NJ: Jason Aronson, 1995).

28. Yochi Brandes, *Akiva's Orchard* (Kinneret, Israel: Zmora-Bitan, 2012).

29. The notion that Akiva was a convert, the son of a convert, or the descendant of a convert was rejected as far back as the 1906 article on Akiva by the great talmudist Louis Ginzberg in the *Jewish Encyclopedia*.

30. Rubenstein, *Stories of the Babylonian Talmud*, 185.

31. *The Tanakh*, 2nd ed. (Philadelphia: Jewish Publication Society, 2000).

Chapter One. Akiva's World

1. There are a number of terms for the geographical area in which Akiva lived. The "Land of Israel" (*Eretz Yisrael* in Hebrew) has biblical origins. "Palestine" is the term that the Romans used. It is usually understood as being derived from the Roman term for Philistine. I will follow common practice and use the various terms interchangeably.

2. The revolts of the Jews included the "Great Revolt"—sometimes called the "First Revolt" or the "First Jewish War"—of 66–70 CE; the "Diaspora Revolt" of 116–117 CE; and the "Bar Kokhba Revolt" of 132–135 CE.

3. See Martin Goodman, "The Pilgrimage Economy of Jerusalem in the Second Temple Period," in Goodman, *Judaism in the Roman World: Selected Essays* (Leiden: Brill, 2007), 59.

4. Seth Schwartz, *Imperialism and Jewish Society: 200 BCE to 640 CE* (Princeton, NJ: Princeton University Press, 2001), 47.

5. Martin Goodman, "The Temple in First-Century CE Judaism," in Goodman, *Judaism in the Roman World*, 47.

6. Lee I. Levine, *The Ancient Synagogue: The First Thousand Years* (New Haven, CT: Yale University Press, 2000), 138.

7. Shaye Cohen, *From the Maccabees to the Mishnah* (Philadelphia: Westminster, 1987), 114–15.

8. Schwartz, *Imperialism*, 49–50.

9. Seth Schwartz, *The Ancient Jews from Alexander to Muhammad* (Cambridge: Cambridge University Press, 2014), 80.

10. Ibid., 86.

11. In Hebrew *rabbanim*; a synonym often used is *hahamim*, literally "the wise ones," conventionally translated into English as "the sages."

12. Seth Schwartz, "The Political Geography of Rabbinic Texts," in *The Cambridge Companion to the Talmud and Rabbinic Literature*, ed. Charlotte Elisheva Fonrobert and Martin S. Jaffee (Cambridge: Cambridge University Press, 2007), 77.

13. Tractate Avot also is known as Pirkei Avot ("Chapters" or "Teachings of the Fathers") and in a slightly altered form appears

in traditional Jewish prayer books. It is one of the most well-known of rabbinic sources, filled with pithy moral statements.

14. Interestingly, a recent article takes a different view about the role of the Avot passage in defining rabbinic historical self-consciousness, but it deals with issues beyond the scope of our concerns here: Adiel Schremer, "*Avot* Reconsidered: Rethinking Rabbinic Judaism," *Jewish Quarterly Review* 105:3 (Summer 2015), 287–311.

15. Josephus mentions a fourth sect as well, but these three are the most prominent. There are likely to have been a number of other sects as well, unmentioned by Josephus.

16. Steven D. Fraade, "Rabbinic Midrash and Ancient Biblical Interpretation," in *The Cambridge Companion*, 100.

17. Shaye Cohen, "The Significance of Yavneh: Pharisees, Rabbis, and the End of Jewish Sectarianism," *Hebrew Union College Annual (HUCA)* 55, 40.

18. Schwartz, "Political Geography of Rabbinic Texts," 77.

19. Schwartz, *Imperialism*, 97–98.

20. Beth A. Berkowitz, *Execution and Invention: Death Penalty Discourse in Early Rabbinic and Christian Cultures* (Oxford: Oxford University Press, 2006), 6.

21. For example, the role of rabbis in synagogues developed slowly and did not really begin to take shape until around the mid-third to fourth centuries CE. See Lee I. Levine, "The Sages and the Synagogue in Late Antiquity," in *The Galilee in Late Antiquity*, ed. Lee I. Levine (New York: Jewish Theological Seminary Press, 1992), 206, 220.

22. Shaye Cohen, "The Place of the Rabbi in Jewish Society of the Second Century," in *The Galilee in Late Antiquity*, 157. The numbers are inexact. Haim Lapin in *Rabbis as Romans* (Oxford: Oxford University Press, 2012), 66–67, has slightly different figures. But the main point remains the same: the number of rabbis at any given time was a good deal smaller than we might have guessed.

23. "The 'urbanization' of rabbis seems to have been a gradual process, just like the urbanization of Palestine," writes Catherine

Hezser, *The Social Structure of the Rabbinic Movement in Roman Palestine* (Tübingen: Mohr Siebeck, 1997), 492.

24. The precise social status of the earliest rabbis is a matter of some debate among scholars, and given the paucity of evidence, it is unlikely that an easy conclusion can ever be determined. Shaye Cohen has argued that they were mostly "well-to-do landowners." See Cohen, "Place of the Rabbi," 169–70. Seth Schwartz views them more as from the "sub-elite" class, "administrators, judges, scribes"; *Ancient Jews*, 108.

25. Finkelstein saw the plebeian scholars' views as being "unheard in the counsels of the great." These views, Finkelstein believed, became what we know as the "oral law"—unrecognized and rejected by the rulers of the people but "accepted as authoritative by large masses." Louis Finkelstein, *Akiba: Scholar, Saint and Martyr* (Philadelphia: Jewish Publication Society, 1936), 31.

26. Cohen, "Place of the Rabbi," 173.

27. David Goodblatt, *Rabbinic Instruction in Sasanian Babylonia* (Leiden: E. J. Brill, 1975), 267.

28. Lapin, *Rabbis as Romans*, 79.

29. Hezser, *Social Structure*, 213–14. See also Jeffrey L. Rubenstein, "Social and Institutional Settings of Rabbinic Literature," in *The Cambridge Companion*, 169.

30. Cohen, "Place of the Rabbi," 160–64.

31. Ibid.

32. Hezser, *Social Structure*, 493.

Chapter Two. A Self-Created Sage

1. Scholars no longer consider rabbinic stories as "reliable historical sources," as Jeffrey L. Rubenstein puts it. See his discussion in *Talmudic Stories: Narrative Art, Composition, and Culture* (Baltimore: Johns Hopkins University Press, 1999), 3.

2. For example, Jonathan Wyn Schofer, *The Making of a Sage: A Study in Rabbinic Ethics* (Madison: University of Wisconsin Press, 2005).

3. The translation here is adapted from the standard English

translation by Judah Goldin, *The Fathers According to Rabbi Nathan* (New York: Schocken, 1955), 41–42.

4. My use of "arcane speech" follows the suggestion of Anthony J. Saldarini, in his translation of Avot de Rabbi Natan Version B, *The Fathers According to Rabbi Nathan (Abot de Rabbi Nathan) Version B: A Translation and Commentary* (Leiden: Brill, 1975), 95 n8.

5. Interestingly, this explanatory line appears in some manuscripts of the text and not in others. Before modernity, Jewish texts were preserved in a variety of manuscripts written by copyists and editors over the course of many years. Often these manuscripts differ in both small and large ways.

6. It recalls a famous midrash (Genesis Rabbah 39:1) in which Abraham discovers the existence of God by asking himself, "Is it conceivable that there is none to look after the world?"

7. That midrash, which mostly deals with the nature of rabbinic authority, is found in the Babylonian Talmud, Hagigah 3a–b.

8. The term *am ha-aretz* was the subject of close examination in a classic scholarly monograph by Aharon Oppenheimer almost forty years ago. Oppenheimer views the term as having two senses in the early Rabbinic Period: a person who does not scrupulously observe certain specific commandments, or a person who is an ignoramus in Torah learning. It is, as he puts it, a "derogatory designation" in either sense of the term. Aharon Oppenheimer, *The Am Ha-Aretz: A Study in the Social History of the Jewish People in the Hellenistic-Roman Period* (Leiden: Brill, 1977), 12.

9. Richard Kalmin, *The Sage in Jewish Society in Late Antiquity* (London: Routledge, 1999), 7–13.

10. In a recent article the scholar Azzan Yadin has done a careful study of the various origin texts and their relationship to one another. See Azzan Yadin, "Rabbi Akiva's Youth," *Jewish Quarterly Review* 100:4 (2010), 573–97.

Chapter Three. A Love Story

1. For example, Rose G. Lurie, *The Great March, Book I* (New York: Union of American Hebrew Congregations, 1931); Morde-

cai H. Lewittes, *Highlights of Jewish History, Vol. 3* (New York: Hebrew Publishing Co., 1955); Ellen Frankel, *The Classic Tales* (Northvale, NJ: Jason Aronson, 1989).

2. Conventionally the phrase I translate as "to study with a rabbi" has been rendered as "to the Beit Midrash," but following recent scholarship (as I discussed in chapter 1), I think it is likely that Akiva was studying not in a formal institution as suggested by "Beit Midrash" but rather at the home or designated room of a rabbi as part of a "disciple circle."

3. Sometimes the term "disinherit" is used to describe what her father did, but according to Jewish law of that period, unless she was an only child, a daughter would not *inherit* property from her father. Rather, Ben Kalba Savua has cut off all economic connection to her.

4. By the Middle Ages the two parts of the marriage process had been merged into one event: *kiddushin* and *nissuin* became part of the same wedding ceremony, as they are today. Note that the other word for wedding is *huppah*, the term for the wedding canopy under which the couple stands, up to our own time.

5. For marriage customs and laws, see Michael L. Satlow, "Marriage and Divorce," in *The Oxford Handbook of Jewish Daily Life in Roman Palestine*, ed. Catherine Hezser (Oxford: Oxford University Press, 2010), 346–52. See also Haim Lapin, *Rabbis as Romans* (Oxford: Oxford University Press, 2012), 133–35.

6. Satlow, "Marriage and Divorce," 350.

7. Some versions say "straw"—perhaps to keep this story connected to the talmudic version of living in the hayloft?—but wood seems to be the preferable reading.

8. Translation here is adapted from Anthony J. Saldarini, *The Fathers According to Rabbi Nathan: Abot De Rabbi Nathan Version B* (Leiden: Brill, 1975), 97.

9. See Satlow, "Marriage and Divorce."

10. Tal Ilan, *Mine and Yours Are Hers: Retrieving Women's History from Rabbinic Literature* (Leiden: Brill, 1997), 182–83.

11. Susan Marks, "Follow That Crown: Or, Rhetoric, Rabbis, and Women Patrons," *Journal of Feminist Studies in Religion* 24:2

(Fall 2008), 77–96. There has been a good deal of scholarship around the "Jerusalem of Gold" term. In addition to the Marks article I have benefited from Shalom Paul, "Jerusalem of Gold—Revisited," in *"I Will Speak the Riddles of Ancient Times": Archeological and Historical Studies in Honor of Amihai Mazar*, ed. Aren M. Maier and Pierre De Miroschedji, Vol. 1 (Winona Lake, IN: Eisenbrauns, 2006), 787–94; and Tziona Grossmark, "A City of Gold: In Quest of Talmudic Reality," *Journal of Jewish Studies* 60:1 (2009), 48–59.

12. Avot de Rabbi Natan (Version A, chapter 6) adds the detail that later in life, in addition to the golden headpiece, Akiva had "golden slippers made for his wife" and that they slept on "beds of gold."

13. For example, b. Sanhedrin 109a and b. Avodah Zarah 17b and 18b.

14. Dafna Shlezinger-Katzman, "Clothing," in Heszer, ed., *Oxford Handbook of Jewish Daily Life*, 372.

15. Ilan, *Mine and Yours Are Hers*, 296.

16. This is a highly abbreviated summation of a complicated academic discussion that has taken place during the past thirty or forty years. Tradition ascribes the editing of the Talmud to two Babylonian rabbis, Rav Ashi and Ravina. The anonymous Stamma'im are understood by scholars today as shaping the Talmud in significant and active ways and are assumed to have flourished at a somewhat later date than the conventional assumptions about the two Babylonian sages. For more on this, see David Weiss Halivni, *The Formation of the Babylonian Talmud*, trans. Jeffrey L. Rubenstein (Oxford: Oxford University Press, 2013).

17. Daniel Boyarin, *Carnal Israel: Reading Sex in Talmudic Culture* (Berkeley: University of California Press, 1993), 136.

18. Ibid., 142.

19. Ibid., 151.

20. Ibid.

21. Shamma Friedman, "A Good Story Deserves Retelling—The Unfolding of the Akiva Legend," *Jewish Studies: An Internet*

Journal 3 (2004), 55–93. This superb article has been very helpful to me in thinking about the Akiva "love story."

22. He is usually known as Rabbenu Nissim, "our rabbi Nissim," or commonly by the acronym of his name, "the RaN," a practice with names typical of many of the great rabbis of the Middle Ages.

23. Nissim of Gerona, Commentary on b. Nedarim, 50b.

Chapter Four. The Growth of a Scholar

1. The historicity is questioned, for example, by the fact that at the time of the siege of Jerusalem, Vespasian was no longer in Palestine and had already returned to Rome with hopes of becoming the new Caesar. His son Titus was in command of the Roman forces at the time of the siege.

2. Haim Lapin, *Rabbis as Romans* (Oxford: Oxford University Press, 2012), 44.

3. Seth Schwartz, *The Ancient Jews from Alexander to Muhammad* (Cambridge: Cambridge University Press, 2014), 118–23.

4. Readers who know Hebrew might be surprised to see the tractate's Hebrew name, Semahot, translated as "Mourning" since the word literally means "Happy Occasions." In fact the volume deals almost exclusively with death and mourning rituals, but as if to stave off bad fortune, a euphemism is used and the text about death is called by a happier name.

5. There are certain exceptions to this rule, not relevant to our case here.

6. A darker take on the story is offered by Daniel Boyarin, "Women's Bodies and the Rise of the Rabbis: The Case of Sotah," in *Jews and Gender: The Challenge to Hierarchy*, ed. Jonathan Frankel (New York: Oxford University Press, 2001), 94–95.

7. Scholars view Song of Songs Rabbah as a mid-sixth-century CE text, but it certainly includes older traditions as well.

8. The translation here is adapted from Baruch M. Bokser and Lawrence H. Schiffman, *The Talmud of the Land of Israel, Vol. 13, Yerushalmi Pesahim* (Chicago: University of Chicago Press,

1994), 273–78. Thanks also to their useful commentary on the interaction.

9. The language in Akiva's prayer—*avinu malkenu*, "our Father, our King"—comes down through the ages as one of the central motifs of the Rosh Hashanah and Yom Kippur liturgy (and the liturgy for other fast days as well).

Chapter Five. Among the Rabbis

1. The Haggadah gets this midrash from the early midrashic text Mekhilta.

2. Though we should also remember that even though the Talmud was compiled some time around the sixth century CE, it drew upon much earlier traditions that in all likelihood had been handed down orally.

3. This is not to say that verbal prayer did not exist before the destruction of the Temple. The singing or recitation of Psalms and other prayers were part of the Temple service, and Jews offered prayers separately from the Temple service as well, though we do not know a great deal about what that liturgy looked like.

4. The *turgeman*, sometimes written *meturgeman*, was a person in the rabbinic academy who has sometimes been called the "living loudspeaker" for the rabbi teaching. It was considered beneath the rabbi's dignity to stand or to shout (in a world without microphones) while he was delivering his discourse. So the *turgeman* stood next to the rabbi and repeated the rabbi's teachings in a loud voice for all to hear. When the sages force Hutzpit to be quiet, it essentially pulled the plug on Rabban Gamaliel's sound system.

5. Shaye Cohen, "The Place of the Rabbi in Jewish Society of the Second Century," in *The Galilee in Late Antiquity*, ed. Lee I. Levine (New York: Jewish Theological Seminary Press, 1992), 173. Akiva presaged the changes that came in the wake of changes put into place many years after his death by Rabbi Judah the Patriarch.

6. Jeffrey L. Rubenstein, *Talmudic Stories: Narrative Art, Composition, and Culture* (Baltimore: Johns Hopkins University Press, 1999), 34–63.

7. Four hundred is in the traditional printed text. Some manuscripts say four rather than four hundred.

8. Translation adapted from Jeffrey L. Rubenstein, *Rabbinic Stories* (Mahwah, NJ: Paulist Press, 2002), 82–83.

9. Ibid., 80.

10. See b. Mo'ed Kattan "Minor Festival" 15a.

11. Rubenstein, *Talmudic Stories*, 44.

12. Ibid., 43.

13. Such as in a famous story in the Babylonian Talmud (Makkot "Punishments" 24b) in which he comforts three other rabbis after they have witnessed a fox running through the ruined Temple's most sacred spot, the Holy of Holies.

14. See b. Mo'ed Kattan 15a.

Chapter Six. In the Orchard

1. In my translation of this story I have left out the typical biblical "proof texts" found in rabbinic literature (hence the ellipses in the quotation), just keeping to the details of the tale. Important elements can be discovered by a careful analysis of the choice of those biblical quotations, but they are of less concern to our enterprise here.

2. The most significant difference is that in the Jerusalem Talmud, unlike the other three versions, it is Ben Zoma who dies and Ben Azzai who "was stricken."

3. For example, Peter Schäfer, *The Origins of Jewish Mysticism* (Princeton, NJ: Princeton University Press, 2009).

4. See Gershom G. Scholem, *Jewish Gnosticism, Merkabah Mysticism, and Talmudic Tradition*, 2nd ed. (New York: Jewish Theological Seminary of America, 1965), 14–19, and Gershom G. Scholem, *Major Trends in Jewish Mysticism* (New York: Schocken, 1946, 1954), 52–53.

5. A recent exploration of these issues can be found in Ra'anan Boustan, "Rabbinization and the Making of Early Jewish Mysticism," *Jewish Quarterly Review* 101:4 (Fall 2011), 482–501.

6. Schäfer, *Origins*, 203.

7. Scholars who have debated the meaning of the story in-

clude E. E. Urbach, David Halperin, and C. R. A. Morray-Jones, among others. Those wishing to further explore this tale can turn to the notes in the opening pages of the fine and lengthy article by Alon Goshen-Gottstein, "Four Entered Paradise Revisited," *Harvard Theological Review* 88:1 (1995), 69–133, in which the scholarship up to 1995 is well-summarized. More recent explorations include Schäfer, *Origins*; Moshe Idel, *Ascensions on High in Jewish Mysticism: Pillars, Lines, Ladders* (Budapest: Central European University Press, 2005); Rachel Elior, *The Three Temples: On the Emergence of Jewish Mysticism* (Portland, OR: Littman Library of Jewish Civilization, 2005); and Martha Himmelfarb, *Between Temple and Torah: Essays on Priests, Scribes, and Visionaries in the Second Temple Period and Beyond* (Tübingen: Mohr Siebeck, 2013).

8. Many different religions, both Eastern and Western, have mystical traditions embedded within them, and although these various mysticisms share certain common features—most significantly a direct encounter with something beyond life as we ordinarily experience it—both the language with which these experiences are described and the nature of the mystical experiences differ profoundly from one religion to the next.

9. One oddity about the early Jewish mystical texts is that even though it is clear that the dominant metaphor is a heavenly ascent, the term used about these mystics is *yordei Merkavah*, those who go *down* to the chariot.

10. The most extensive treatment of the traditions about Elisha ben Abuya is the fine book by Alon Goshen-Gottstein, *The Sinner and the Amnesiac: The Rabbinic Invention of Elisha ben Abuya and Eleazar ben Arach* (Stanford, CA: Stanford University Press, 2000).

11. See ibid., 69, for example.

12. Schäfer, *Origins*, 203.

13. David J. Halperin, *The Merkabah in Rabbinic Literature* (New Haven, CT: American Oriental Society, 1980), 88.

14. Jewish tradition asserts that through knowing the secret names of God, one can attain mystical or even magical results. We see this much later in Jewish tradition with the famous story of the

golem of Prague. In the Hekhalot literature Rabbi Akiva "is described as receiving the revelation of a name while contemplating the vision of the divine chariot"—Idel, *Ascensions on High*, 31.

15. Halperin, *Merkabah*, 88; Idel, *Ascensions on High*, 32.

16. C. R. A. Morray-Jones, "Paradise Revisited (2 Cor 12:1–12): The Jewish Mystical Background of Paul's Apostolate, Part 1: The Jewish Sources," *Harvard Theological Review* 86 (1993), 177–217.

17. Goshen-Gottstein, "Four Entered Paradise," 104.

18. Ibid.

19. Idel, *Ascensions on High*, 30–31.

20. The whole text is translated in Morray-Jones, "Paradise Revisited," 196–98.

21. Schäfer, *Origins*, 285.

22. Ibid., 287.

23. Ibid., 290.

24. Goshen-Gottstein, "Four Entered Paradise," 129.

Chapter Seven. The Last Years

1. See b. Semahot 8:13 and b. Mo'ed Kattan 21b.

2. In b. Bekhorot "First Things" 58a, Ben Azzai in a moment of disdain about his colleagues says, "All the sages of Israel compared to me are like the shell of a garlic, except for that bald one." (Of course later commentators dispute that he is really referring to Akiva with such a disrespectful appellation.)

3. See b. Yevamot "Levirate Marriage" 63b. The Babylonian Talmud in Tractate Shabbat 156b tells a story about how his daughter is saved from being bitten by a snake on her wedding day, thanks to an act of charity that she performed the evening before.

4. For more on this time, see, for example, Martin Goodman, *Judaism in the Roman World: Selected Essays* (Leiden: Brill, 2007), 52.

5. Ibid., 53.

6. Moshe Halbertal, in his insightful book *On Sacrifice* (Princeton, NJ: Princeton University Press, 2012), 37–62, discusses the "substitution" of charity or suffering for sacrifices in some detail.

7. Baruch Bokser, *The Origins of the Seder* (Berkeley: University of California Press, 1984), 92.

8. Goodman, *Judaism*, 53.

9. Ibid.

10. The name combines a version of Hadrian's family name, Aelius, with a reference to the three Roman gods (Jupiter, Juna, and Minerva) worshipped in the Temple of Jupiter Optimus Maximus (literally, "Jupiter, the best and greatest") on the Capitoline Hill in Rome.

11. Seth Schwartz, *The Ancient Jews from Alexander to Muhammad* (Cambridge: Cambridge University Press, 2014), 93.

12. Martin Goodman, "Trajan and the Origins of the Bar Kokhba War," in Peter Schäfer, ed., *The Bar Kokhba War Reconsidered* (Tübingen: Mohr Siebeck, 2003), 28.

13. And in fact the ban may have had nothing to do with the Jews specifically. Schwartz points out that "Egyptian priests and various Arab groups also practiced circumcision, and the prohibition applied to all. The law against circumcision may have been a coincidence" (*Ancient Jews*, 97).

14. Peter Schäfer, "Preface," in Schäfer, ed., *Bar Kokhba War Reconsidered*, viii.

15. Schäfer gives a good summary of everything we don't know in Schäfer, ed., *Bar Kokhba War Reconsidered*, vii–viii.

16. The word "bar" in Aramaic is equivalent to "ben" (son) in Hebrew. It is familiar to us today from the term Bar Mitzvah.

17. Peter Schäfer, "Bar Kokhba and the Rabbis," in Schäfer, ed., *Bar Kokhba War Reconsidered*, 15.

18. Hanan Eshel, "The Bar Kokhba Revolt, 132–135," in *The Cambridge History of Judaism*, Vol. 4, ed. Steven T. Katz (Cambridge: Cambridge University Press, 2008), 110.

19. Schäfer, "Bar Kokhba and the Rabbis," 9.

20. Schwartz, *Ancient Jews*, 94.

21. Eshel, "Bar Kokhba Revolt," 123.

22. Ibid., 126–27.

23. Gershom Scholem, "Toward an Understanding of the Mes-

sianic Idea in Judaism," in *The Messianic Idea in Judaism and other Essays on Jewish Spirituality* (Schocken Books, 1971), 3–7, *passim*.

24. Schäfer, "Bar Kokhba and the Rabbis," 18.

25. Ibid., 21.

26. "Diphtheria" is the scholarly view of the meaning of the Hebrew word *askharah;* older translations often use "croup."

27. Aaron Amit, "The Death of Rabbi Akiva's Disciples: A Literary History," *Journal of Jewish Studies* 56:2 (Autumn 2005), 265–84. I draw upon Amit's excellent work about the history of the story in some of my comments here. Amit cites the connection to the ruling of R. Natronai forbidding celebrations.

28. Ibid., 270.

29. Ibid.

30. Jeffrey L. Rubenstein, *Talmudic Stories: Narrative Art, Composition, and Culture* (Baltimore: Johns Hopkins University Press, 1999), 3.

31. See, for example, the very different readings by Daniel Boyarin, *Dying for God: Martyrdom and the Making of Christianity and Judaism* (Palo Alto, CA: Stanford University Press, 1999), who sees the tale as "a story of contention over martyrdom between Rabbinic and Christian Jews" (p. 103); and Paul Mandel, "Was Rabbi Aqiva a Martyr?," in *Rabbinic Traditions between Palestine and Babylonia*, ed. Ronit Nikolsky and Tal Ilan (Leiden: Brill, 2014), 306–53, who reads the story as not being about martyrdom at all. See also the reading by Michael Fishbane, *The Kiss of God: Spiritual and Mystical Death in Judaism* (Seattle: University of Washington Press, 1994), 66–81. Mandel has a footnote early on in his article listing some of the major scholarship on these tales (p. 308 n4).

32. The Shema as it appears in a prayer book is composed of three sections, each a biblical passage: Deuteronomy 6:4–9, Deuteronomy 11:13–21, and Numbers 15:37–41, in that order. Our focus here is on only the first section.

33. Of course Akiva lived about a century before the completion of the Mishnah. The Talmud here seems to attribute the Mishnah's understanding of the Shema to Akiva, though in the

Mishnah itself the interpretation is unattributed to any particular teacher.

34. Aaron Oppenheimer, "The Ban on Circumcision as a Cause of the Revolt: A Reconsideration," in Schäfer, ed., *Bar Kokhba War Reconsidered*, 68. Oppenheimer's article shows that the ban on circumcision did not precede the revolt but came afterwards and therefore was not a cause for the uprising.

35. Schwartz, *Ancient Jews*, 96–97.

36. Boyarin, *Dying for God*, 103.

37. Ibid. At the same time Boyarin says that "there is not a lot of evidence" that Pappus "is a figure for a Christian."

38. Louis Finkelstein, *Akiba: Scholar, Saint and Martyr* (Philadelphia: Jewish Publication Society, 1936), 274.

39. Beth A. Berkowitz, *Execution and Invention: Death Penalty Discourse in Early Rabbinic and Christian Cultures* (Oxford: Oxford University Press, 2006), 154–55.

40. The "heavenly voice" (in Hebrew *bat kol*) is a device that is typically used in rabbinic literature to indicate, more or less, God's own point of view. It is one step removed from hearing the actual voice of God—such as at the revelation at Sinai—but it is very close.

41. This is first explored in m. Berakhot, chapter 2, and then discussed at length in b. Berakhot 13a and forward.

42. Mandel, "Was Rabbi Aqiva a Martyr?," 320–32.

43. Fishbane, *Kiss of God*, 67.

44. Translation adapted from Mandel, "Was Rabbi Aqiva a Martyr?," 313.

45. Ibid., 318.

46. Ibid., 334. This same image of Akiva the teacher is mirrored by various stories about his time in jail. Various students—Rabbi Joshua Habarsi, Rabbi Yohanan the Cobbler, Rabbi Shimon bar Yohai—come to learn from him as he awaits his trial.

47. Fishbane, *Kiss of God*, 73.

48. Scholars are not sure whether the poem is based on the Midrash of the Ten Martyrs itself or on some other source. Nothing is known about the author of the poem, though it is sometimes

assumed that his name was Yehudah Hazak, taking the first letters of the opening verses as an authorial acrostic. This may or may not be historically accurate.

49. Fishbane, *Kiss of God*, 71.

Epilogue. The Afterlife of Akiva

1. Richard Kalmin, "Patterns and Developments in Rabbinic Midrash of Late Antiquity," in *Hebrew Bible/Old Testament: The History of Its Interpretation*, Vol. 1, ed. Magne Saebo (Göttingen: Vandenhoeck & Ruprecht, 1996), 290.

2. Almost the exact same story is told in the early midrash Sifre on Deuteronomy (Piska 41). There the discussion also takes place in the town of Lod but in the "upper story" of the house of a different person (named Aris), and a third rabbi is also part of the conversation. Otherwise, the conclusion remains the same. In the classic Soncino English translation of the Talmud, the line attributed to Rabbi Akiva is "study is greater *because it leads to practice*." But in the Hebrew the sentence reads only "study is greater," without any reason given. Why Soncino chose to add the explanatory phrase is unclear to me. At any rate the version in midrash Sifre Deuteronomy quotes Akiva as saying study is greater without any "because."

3. That story is found in Sanhedrin 74a where the rabbis are reported to have gathered to vote on a fascinating question: Is a person permitted to violate the commandments of the Torah if he or she is presented with the threat "transgress this law of the Torah or you will be killed."

4. For more information on "reclining" at the Seder and its place in the Greco-Roman world of the rabbis, see the detailed commentary by Joshua Kulp, *The Schechter Haggadah: Art, History and Commentary* (Jerusalem: Schechter Institute of Jewish Studies, 2009), 174–79.

5. For more on this tension, see Norman Lamm, *Torah Lishmah: Study of Torah for Torah's Sake in the Work of Rabbi Hayyim Volozhin and His Contemporaries* (New York: Ktav, 1989), 138–90. See also the interesting discussion in Michael Rosenak, *Roads to the Palace* (Providence: Berghahn, 1995) 231–34.

6. We have already seen in chapter 6 Akiva's importance for early Merkavah mysticism, but that influence continued. For example, see Lawrence Fine's major biography of Rabbi Isaac Luria, the great mystic of sixteenth-century Safed, *Physician of the Soul, Healer of the Cosmos: Isaac Luria and His Kabbalistic Fellowship* (Stanford, CA: Stanford University Press, 2003), 330–35.

7. Surprisingly to our ears, the typical expression in rabbinic literature for having holy status is that the books "defile the hands." The expression seems to be associated with the idea that physically touching these books connects one directly to the sacred, a dangerous and special order of reality. Akiva uses this expression in his argument in favor of the Song of Songs. The expression is discussed in Sid Z. Leiman, *The Canonization of Hebrew Scripture: The Talmudic and Midrashic Evidence* (Hamden, CT: Archon, 1976), and more recently in Shamma Friedman, "The Holy Scriptures Defile the Hands—The Transformation of a Biblical Concept in Rabbinic Theology," in *Minhah Le-Nahum: Biblical and Other Studies Presented to Nahum M. Sarna in Honour of His 70th Birthday,* ed. Marc Zvi Brettler and Michael Fishbane (Sheffield: Sheffield Academic Press, 1993), 117–32. Friedman's convincing (though highly technical for the general reader) argument explores the transformation of the concept from its biblical context to its use in rabbinic sources.

8. This phrase ("are not equal to the day") can be translated in several ways. The classic Soncino translation of the Mishnah renders it, "For the whole world is not as worthy as the day on which the Song of Songs was given to Israel." Or one could translate it as "not worth the day." I am following the version of Michael Fishbane, *JPS Commentary to the Song of Songs* (Philadelphia: Jewish Publication Society, 2015), xxii.

9. The biblical scholar Marc Brettler has written a clear and concise essay summarizing what scholars currently believe about the process: "The Canonization of the Bible," in *The Jewish Study Bible,* ed. Adele Berlin and Marc Zvi Brettler (Oxford: Oxford University Press, 2004).

10. Fishbane, *JPS Commentary,* xxii.

11. This statement, among others about the Song of Songs, is discussed in Arthur Green, "The Song of Songs in Early Jewish Mysticism," in *The Heart of the Matter: Studies in Jewish Mysticism and Theology* (Philadelphia: Jewish Publication Society, 2015), 101–15.

12. See Günter Stemberger's discussion of the origins of the Mishnah in H. L. Strack and Günter Stemberger, *Introduction to the Talmud and Midrash* (Minneapolis: Fortress, 1996), 124–38, quotation from p. 131.

13. The midrashic texts usually associated with the "school of Akiva" include the Mekhilta de Rabbi Shimon bar Yohai, the Sifra on Leviticus, and the Sifre on Deuteronomy; texts usually associated with the "school of Yishmael" include the Mekhilta de Rabbi Yishmael and the Sifre on Numbers.

14. Strack and Stemberger, *Introduction*, 250, point out that the reader "would need to be aware of the purely pragmatic (not historical) nature of this nomenclature."

15. My own view is that the best analysis of the core questions can be found in Menahem I. Kahana, "The Halakhic Midrashim," in *The Literature of the Sages, Part Two*, ed. Shmuel Safrai, Zeev Safrai, Joshua Schwartz, and Peter J. Tomson (Minneapolis: Fortress, 2006), particularly 3–40. But this book is difficult to find and assumes an advanced knowledge of rabbinic terminology. Other works that address the questions similarly are aimed at scholars: Jay Harris, *How Do We Know This?* (Albany: SUNY Press, 1995), 25–72; Kalmin, "Patterns and Developments"; and most recently Azzan Yadin-Israel, *Scripture and Tradition: Rabbi Akiva and the Triumph of Midrash* (Philadelphia: University of Pennsylvania Press, 2015). For the general reader the best summary can be found in Strack and Stemberger, *Introduction*, 247–51. This is Stemberger's updating of a classic work by Strack that first appeared in English in 1931. Older editions of the book without Stemberger's updating can still be found but should be avoided.

16. Heschel wrote the book in Hebrew, and it appeared in the early 1960s in three volumes (the third published after Heschel's death). The book remained untranslated for decades. Finally, a

monumental English translation appeared a decade ago, including both Heschel's footnotes and explanatory notes and commentary by the translators: *Heavenly Torah: As Refracted through the Generations*, ed. and trans. with commentary by Gordon Tucker with Leonard Levin (New York: Continuum, 2005).

17. Ibid., xxviii, xxix.

18. See, for example, the discussion in Shai Held, *Abraham Joshua Heschel: The Call of Transcendence* (Bloomington: Indiana University Press, 2013), 161.

19. Heschel, *Heavenly Torah*, 40, 45.

20. Kahana, "Halakhic Midrashim," 18, 21, 26, 21.

21. Jeffrey L. Rubenstein, *Rabbinic Stories* (New York: Paulist, 2002), 217.

22. Jeffrey L. Rubenstein, *Stories of the Babylonian Talmud* (Baltimore: Johns Hopkins University Press, 2010), 186–87.

23. Azzan Yadin-Israel, *Scripture and Tradition*, 178.

24. Margaret Atwood, *MaddAddam* (New York: Anchor, 2014), 56.

25. Steven I. Zipperstein, *Elusive Prophet: Ahad Ha'am and the Origins of Zionism* (Berkeley: University of California Press, 1993), 213, 214.

26. My translation here tries to be closer to the original than the standard English edition, *Ahad Ha-Am: Essays, Letters, Memoirs*, ed. and trans. Leon Simon (Philadelphia: Jewish Publication Society, 1912). Various editions are in print today.

27. On the matter of the multiple voices in rabbinic discourse, see, for example, Steven D. Fraade, "Rabbinic Polysemy and Pluralism Revisited: Between Praxis and Thematization," *Association for Jewish Studies (AJS) Review* 31:1 (2007), 31–37.

INDEX OF SUBJECTS

INDEX OF PRIMARY SOURCES

Hebrew Bible

Genesis
   5:1–2, 174–75
Exodus
   8:15, 108
   14:31, 108
   23:2, 124
Leviticus
   19:17–18, 100
   19:18, 174–75
   21, 87
   22:31, 113–14
   23:2, 113–14
   23:4, 111–14
Numbers
   15:37–41, 209 n32
   24:17, 150
Deuteronomy
   6:4–5, 160–62, 166–67, 171
   11:13–21, 209 n32
   30:12, 123
   30:20, 162

Judges
   9:38, 93
2 Kings
   2:11, 65–66
   2:12, 129
Psalms
   23:1, 75
   95:8, 42–43
   101:7, 139, 143
   104:24, 79
   148:7–14, 135
Job
   14:19, 39–42, 45
   28:9–11, 48–49, 53–54
Proverbs
   9:8, 99, 101
   12:10, 68, 70, 74–75
   29:7, 75
Song of Songs
   1:4, 141–43
Ecclesiastes
   11:6, 157–58

Minor Tractates

JEWISH LIVES is a major series of interpretive
biography designed to illuminate the imprint of Jewish
figures upon literature, religion, philosophy, politics, cultural
and economic life, and the arts and sciences. Subjects are
paired with authors to elicit lively, deeply informed books that
explore the range and depth of Jewish experience
from antiquity through the present.

Jewish Lives is a partnership of Yale University Press
and the Leon D. Black Foundation.

Ileene Smith is editorial director. Anita Shapira and
Steven J. Zipperstein are series editors.

Moses Mendelssohn: Sage of Modernity, by Shmuel Feiner
Moses: A Human Life, by Avivah Zornberg
Proust: The Search, by Benjamin Taylor
Yitzhak Rabin: Soldier, Leader, Statesman, by Itamar Rabinovich
Walter Rathenau: Weimar's Fallen Statesman, by Shulamit Volkov
Mark Rothko: Toward the Light in the Chapel,
    by Annie Cohen-Solal
Solomon: The Lure of Wisdom, by Steven Weitzman
Steven Spielberg: A Life in Films, by Molly Haskell
Barbra Streisand: Redefining Beauty, Femininity, and Power,
    by Neal Gabler
Leon Trotsky: A Revolutionary's Life, by Joshua Rubenstein